The FRIENDSHIP BOOK

of Francis Gay

D. C. THOMSON & CO., LTD.
London Glasgow Manchester Dundee

A Thought
For Each Day
In 1985

We pass this way but once,
so smell the flowers on the way.

SEA SYMPHONY

JANUARY

TUESDAY—JANUARY 1.

I WONDER how many of us manage to keep a diary. Many people seem to keep it going for a week or two at the most and then give up. Perhaps they try to write too much—or leave it for several days and then forget what has happened.

I once knew someone who had a simpler form of diary-keeping which she managed to sustain through the year. Each day she recorded, in just two or three words, something good which had happened to her that day. It could be the simplest of things like "Letter from Mary"; "Back-ache better"; "First crocuses"; "Invitation to John's for Easter"; "A rainbow this evening"; "Fog all gone" and so on. Looking back through her diaries she always finds she has had a "Happy Old Year".

Worth trying, isn't it?

WEDNESDAY—JANUARY 2.

THEY tell a story in the Isle of Anglesey in North Wales of two saints who lived at opposite ends of the island—St Cybi of Holyhead and St Seiriol of Penmon. Each, when they wanted to meet, would journey half-way across the island to a central meeting point. Seiriol, travelling with his back to the sun in the morning and returning in the evening, was called Seiriol the Pale, while his fellow-saint, who faced the sun in both directions, was known as Cybi the Tanned!

A delightful story in its own right, I think, but a reminder too, perhaps, that friendship needs a bit of effort on both sides.

THE FRIENDSHIP BOOK

THE American educationalist, Professor Henry N. Wieman, used to love to tell how a fellow-student of his college days bought himself a special chair equipped with an adjustable book-rest and lamp and he placed a revolving bookshelf within easy reach. He felt that he could study effectively only if he were comfortable, so he bought some soft slippers, a lounging jacket and an eye-shade.

After the college evening meal, said Dr Wieman, the student went to his room. " He took off his coat and put on the jacket, put on his slippers, adjusted the lamp, placed his book on the book-rest, sat down, fitted the eye-shade—and went to sleep!"

How often we think that if only circumstances were right we could do this, or that, or the other. The simple truth is that the *will* to do something is always more important than the circumstances we try to arrange for ourselves.

TOWARDS the end of last century one of the most influential religious speakers in Scotland and beyond was in fact a Professor of Science, Henry Drummond, who held the Chair of Natural Science at the Free Church College at Glasgow.

He helped Moody and Sankey in their first Scottish campaign, preached in the slums and addressed religious meetings for university students.

Scholar though he was he had a simple message and a simple style, an epigramatic way of putting things. One student who went along expecting a theological discourse came away saying, " I'll never forget one sentence he used: ' When the outlook is bad, try the up-look!' "

SATURDAY—JANUARY 5.

I HEARD recently of the owner of a general store who found a gentler way of nudging his customers' memories when they had forgotten to pay their bills than by sending them the usual curt reminder note. He enclosed another copy of the bill and clipped to it a packet of forget-me-not seeds!

He says that this method hardly ever failed, whereas before, he often had to send several reminders. I'm not surprised. Who could resist such a pleasant hint?

SUNDAY—JANUARY 6.

THE heavens declare the glory of God; and the firmament sheweth his handywork.

MONDAY—JANUARY 7.

ONE dark winter night, the Lady of the House and I accepted an invitation to our local church Youth Club where the young people were presenting a " Pageant of Light ". There was a whole series of tableaux including, I remember, a primitive camp-fire scene, a Roman scene with flickering pottery lamps, Florence Nightingale—the Lady of the Lamp, Sir Humphrey Davy inventing his miner's safety lamp, and much besides. Then we came out into the street, lit by bright neon lights . . . and high above, the softer light of moon and stars.

How much we take it for granted . . . the light of a new day, a gleam of sunlight, the soft glow of a lamp, the flicker of firelight, the brightly-lit shop windows, a distant vista at night with street lights strung across like golden beads.

Life is one long " Pageant of Light ".

WONDERLAND

Winter is an artist
 Cunning as can be,
Touching with a magic brush
 Every bush and tree,
Changing into fantasy
 All the world we know.
None but dullards would declare
 '' It's only frost and snow.''

TUESDAY—JANUARY 8.

ANGELA RIPPON, the television personality, has a great love for the Dartmoor countryside in which she has her home. " It's so peaceful down here," she says. " Not quiet—the birdsong and the rush and the chuckle of the water fill the picture with too much sound for it ever to be quiet, but it *is* peaceful."

We often hear people say that they long for a " bit of peace and quiet," yet they are really two quite different things.

In many " peaceful " country places we might hear the lowing of cattle, the cawing of rooks, even the hum of traffic on a distant road. Yet the sounds somehow form a part of our peace.

Silence is an outward thing while peace is inward. Some find it in music, some in the countryside, some in worship and in many another way. But it is peace we need—not just quiet, which can be a very lonely thing.

WEDNESDAY—JANUARY 9.

AWAY back in the 16th century, a certain Dr Nowel served as Dean of St Paul's Cathedral for 44 years. He was 95 when he died, and his epitaph tells us that " His age had neither impaired his hearing, nor dimmed his eyes, nor weakened his memory."

He believed in the old practice of tithing and gave a tenth of his income to charities. But he had another very rigid rule—he gave a " tithe " of his time, too, to recreation! I wonder if this was, in part at any rate, the secret of his long and vigorous life?

We believe in " work well done," but don't let us ever forget the importance of " leisure well spent."

THE FRIENDSHIP BOOK

BROWSING through the index of my dictionary of quotations I was astonished to find that there was not a single reference to " scent " or " fragrance." I tried " smell " and drew a blank there, too!

It is surprising, when you think about it, that our poets and writers go into ecstasies about sights that delight the eye and sounds which gladden the ear, and yet seem to have so little to say about the pleasure which can come through our sense of smell. Perhaps we tend to neglect it ourselves.

I suppose people who wouldn't turn a hair if we said we were going sightseeing would think us pretty odd if we said we were going to have " a smelling day "! But here are some of the delights I discovered when I determined to do just that:

The scent of soap, the aroma of coffee, newly-polished furniture, newly-ironed clothes, roses, new-mown grass, a baker's shop, a chemist's shop, a fruiterer's. It certainly gave a new dimension to my day. You try it!

PERHAPS you have never heard of an ergograph? Then let me tell you that it is an instrument devised to measure fatigue and it was used by a Dr Henry Goddard in his New Jersey training school.

When an assistant said to a tired child at the instrument: " You're doing fine, Johnny," the boy's energy-curve would soar. Discouragement and fault-finding were found to have a measurable opposite effect.

You see, praise is a genuine tonic. It not only pleases the recipient, but triggers off fresh energy as well.

THE DEEP

There's something wild and strange
    About the restless sea,
Its moods that quickly change,
    Its movements fierce and free;
But while in awe we view
    Its majesty and might,
We see its beauty, too,
    And greet it with delight.

SATURDAY—JANUARY 12.

I'M told that the following notice was seen outside a barber's shop in the Norfolk village of Stalham:
This shop is closed all week
unless it is open.
Don't waste time waiting.

SUNDAY—JANUARY 13.

I CAME not to call the righteous, but sinners to repentance.

MONDAY—JANUARY 14.

MARY is getting on a bit now, and she is crippled with rheumatism. She has great difficulty in getting about, but one thing she will never miss if at all possible is the service at her church.

A neighbour once said to her, " I am surprised that you struggle along there when you could watch the service on the television."

Mary admitted that one day she had felt like that herself, but as it was a special missionary service at church she decided to make the effort. She told her neighbour how the missionary had described a little isolated church in Africa where at the end of the service at night each member of the congregation lit their lamps from one in the church porch to light them on the way home.

" It made me realise just *why* I struggle to church," said Mary. " I always bring back something—a thought from the sermon, the refrain of a hymn, a word of greeting from the minister or from others in the church, the echo of a prayer—but it is always something which lights the way home and the rest of the week for me."

TUESDAY—JANUARY 15.

IN his " Life of Noel Coward ", Cole Leslie tells of a train journey which the great actor took in Italy when he was a young man. Leslie recalls, " Travelling by train always excited him, or rather he brought an excitement to it so that the undertaking became an adventure more than just a journey."

How many ordinary everyday things there are—a journey, a walk, a shopping trip, a visit to a friend—which could become adventures if, like Noel Coward we brought excitement to them by joyful anticipation instead of taking them all for granted.

WEDNESDAY—JANUARY 16.

SIR ARTHUR HELPS, the essayist and historian, wrote these lines:
It is hard:
To forget;
To apologise;
To save money;
To be unselfish;
To avoid mistakes;
To keep out of a rut;
To begin all over again;
To make the best of all things;
To keep your temper at all times;
To think first and act afterwards;
To maintain a high standard;
To keep on keeping on;
To shoulder blame;
To be charitable;
To admit error;
To take advice;
To forgive.
    —*But it pays!*

DR ROBERT J. McCRACKEN who was for many years minister of the great Riverside Church in New York, has told how, when he first went to the city, nothing got him down so much as the crowds, " especially the crowds on the subway. To see them at the rush hour in the evening, a swarming, jostling, work-weary multitude, was a depressing business."

He spoke of this to a fellow minister who had spent many years in the city and who confessed that his own early experience had been just the same. Then one day, as he stood strap-hanging on the underground, it struck him that his upraised hand was like a hand raised in benediction. " I began to say to myself, these men and women are my brothers and sisters and life is pressing hard on them. What better can I do than offer a prayer for them?"

Prayer is not just for church and chapel nor even for our private room. Remember the words of William Cowper's hymn:

Where'er we seek Thee, Thou art found,
And every place is hallowed ground.

FRANCISCO GOYA, the Spanish painter, was one of the determined and courageous people who mastered some of the disabilities of growing old. He had such bad eyesight in his old age that others had to sharpen his pencils for him. Despite this he produced some marvellous drawings.

One of his last pictures shows an old, bearded man, bent over and supporting himself on two sticks. The title given to it by Goya, " Aun Aprendo ", shows clearly his philosophy of life. It means, " I am still learning." A great motto for young or old!

SNAP!

I've taken all the family,
*   Our spaniel and the cat.*
Why is it all the grown-ups say
*   " But I don't look like that!"?*

THE FRIENDSHIP BOOK

THE anniversary preacher had taken ill shortly before the service and a deputy had stepped in at short notice. Glancing up at one of the church windows which had been broken and replaced temporarily by a sheet of hardboard the preacher said, " I am afraid I am only a substitute—rather like that piece of hardboard filling in for the stained glass."

He was very amused when, after the service, an old lady came up to him and said, " You're no substitute window, lad. You're a *proper pane!*"

AND when they had brought their ships to land, they forsook all, and followed him.

SOME years ago, the ancient Halifax Piece Hall, where merchants used to bring their cloth for sale, was cleaned and restored and made the site of a museum, art gallery, open-air market and craft shops. In one of the latter the Lady of the House and I came across a wall plaque with an anonymous verse particularly appropriate to the Piece Hall with its associations with the textile trade, but also containing this message of inspiration:

> *Not till the looms are silent and the shuttles cease to fly*
> *Will God unroll the canvas and reveal the reason why*
> *The dark threads are as needful in the weaver's skilful hand*
> *As the threads of gold and silver in the pattern He has planned.*

MANY thousands of people visit Haworth Parsonage every year. I wonder how many of them notice the sampler worked by Miss Elizabeth Branwell—the " Aunt Branwell " of the Brontës who financed their first book of poems with her legacy and who had earlier ruled the Parsonage when Charlotte, Emily, Anne and Branwell were young.

There is no indication in which year Aunt Branwell embroidered the sampler, but it measures $20\frac{1}{2}$ inches by $8\frac{1}{2}$ inches and has a border design. This is its wording:

Charity decent, easy modest kind
Softens the high and rears the abject mind
Not soon provoked,
She easily forgives and much she suffers
As she much believes. Soft peace she brings
Where-ever she arrives she builds our quiet
As she forms our lives, lays the rough paths
Of peevish nature even
And opens in each heart a little heaven.

SOME years ago, in a broadcast service, a preacher told how, in the course of his pastoral visitation, he used to call on the lighthouse-keeper at Lismore in the Firth of Lorne. One day the keeper said to him, " Look down. That's where three tidal currents meet — it's completely still!" And it was true—all around was the turmoil of many waters, but in the centre, peace!

That can be a parable of our lives as it has been in the lives of a multitude of people who have found that spiritual resources of faith, prayer and hope have given them a place of peace amid the turmoil of life.

THE FRIENDSHIP BOOK

"I WISH I were older!" sighs a teenager. " I wish I were younger!" says an old man. Some people are never content at any age. The poet, Carolyn Wells, had no time for youth or old age. She wrote:

> *Youth is a silly vapid state;*
> *Old age with fears and ills is rife;*
> *This simple boon I beg of Fate—*
> *A thousand years of Middle Life!*

Isn't it true that all stages of life have their own special blessings? Whichever one we are at now, let's enjoy it and be grateful for its gifts.

I REMEMBER a snippet of an old poem which speaks of " heroes the world has never known ". These words came to mind again when, on holiday, the Lady of the House and I were wandering round the churchyard at Arncliffe in the Yorkshire Dales.

We saw the grave of a local parson, the Rev. Thomas Lindley, who for 60 years was vicar of the two churches at Halton Gill and Hubberholme hardly ever missing a service at his two churches summer and winter, though Halton Gill was six miles across the fells from Hubberholme. Then there were pastoral calls to outlying farms . . . all this till he died at the age of 93!

I don't suppose people outside his own locality had ever heard of Thomas Lindley and I am certain he would never think of himself as a hero. Yet he is only one of multitudes of folk—not just parsons—simple, humble folk who quietly live out their days faithfully and patiently accomplishing their work in the place where they are set. *I* call them heroes—though the world has never heard of them.

THE FRIENDSHIP BOOK

IT was towards the end of January and a bleak and dreary day, but as I entered the hall where a Brownie Guide meeting was in progress, the chill weather was banished in a flash, for here all was bustle and happy laughter. The girls were as busy as bees, sorting out small items of grocery, packets of sweets, and putting them into separate bags; another group were sorting magazines and paperbacks and adding them to the bags; another group taking the filled bags, tying them up and labelling them.

" My goodness, what a hive of industry!" I said. " What's going on?"

" These are Remembrance Parcels," said one Brownie. " It was Brown Owl's idea."

Jenny, a Sixer, explained: " Brown Owl said that a lot of older people got parcels and visits at Christmas, but then they feel forgotten when Christmas is over, so we thought we'd give them a surprise present to show them they're not forgotten after all."

Bless you, girls!

WITH the merciful thou wilt shew thyself merciful; with an upright man thou wilt shew thyself upright.

THE Very Rev. Fenton Morley, Dean of Salisbury, once said: " There has been a relation between money and religion ever since Noah. He was the only man able to float a company when the rest of the world was in liquidation."

THE FRIENDSHIP BOOK

A CRITIC of Haydn's church music once suggested to the composer that it was not as solemn as it might be for its purpose. This was Haydn's reply:

"I cannot make my church music other than cheerful. I write according to the thoughts I feel. When I think upon God my heart is so full of joy that the notes dance and leap, as it were, from my pen. Since God has given me a cheerful heart I am sure He expects me to serve Him with a cheerful spirit."

DOWN Your Way", the second-longest running radio programme of all time, after "Desert Island Discs", must have brought delight to countless thousands of people since it started in 1946.

To celebrate the 1500th edition, a book was published gathering together interesting extracts from the series. In the introduction to the book Brian Johnson, one of the presenters, wrote: "The papers these days are full of stories about criminals and vandals, and of how selfish and uncaring our society has become. But if you were to come with us round the country on our journeys for 'Down Your Way,' you would, I think, be pleasantly surprised to find how many people are doing things to *help* others."

I LIKE the story of the celebrated Maori who was speaking at a banquet in Wellington.

He said: "People often ask me to what I attribute my success in life. I tell them that my great-grandfather ate the very first Presbyterian missionary to land in New Zealand and I attribute my success to the Scottish blood in my veins!"

FEBRUARY

FRIDAY—FEBRUARY 1.

I HAD to look twice at a title in our local bookshop. It was " How to Complain! " My first thought was that there were plenty of people who didn't need such advice! Actually, the book could be quite useful, for it dealt with dozens of areas of frustration — misleading advertisements, lost luggage, noisy neighbours, computer errors and so on, instructing the reader how to make his or her dissatisfaction known in the proper quarter.

Yet when all that has been said, I come back to my first thought that what a lot of us need is advice how *not* to complain! How much happier we should all be if we could say with St Paul, " I have learned in whatsoever state I find myself therein to be content."

SATURDAY—FEBRUARY 2.

THROUGH the centuries various customs with candles have marked this Candlemas Day. At one time in England families would light an extra-large candle and sit feasting round it till it had burnt away.

I remember one of Tolstoy's stories about a ploughman who took a lighted candle from the church and placed it on his plough to remind himself that " to work is to pray ".

We may not be able—nor may we want—to take a lighted candle to work, but what a difference it could make to our ordinary, everyday life if there was the glow of faith, hope and love at every work-bench, every kitchen-sink, every office-desk, every shop-counter. Work could be transformed for us.

JESUS went out into a mountain to pray, and continued all night in prayer to God.

OVERLOOKING Saltaire Park, Shipley, Bradford, stands a statue of Sir Titus Salt. He built the model mill and village in the mid-19th century when many mill-owners did not care how or where their workers lived, so long as they laboured hard and long.

Sir Titus was so well loved that after his death a little song, " The Saltaire Anthem ", was often sung in his honour:

Peace be to the dust
Of that man so good and just
Whose equal there is none that can compare:
May he live for evermore
On that bright and golden shore.
May angels bless the founder of Saltaire.

Sir Titus transformed the bleak lives of his workers, both in the mill and in their homes and recreations. He deserves to be remembered.

SOPRANO Isobel Baillie delighted audiences everywhere she went with her beautiful singing. Perhaps one of the secrets of her wide appeal was that she put into practice the advice she so often gave to other singers: " Never sing louder than lovely."

I think this applies to many things besides singing. There is much that is noisy and strident in our world and I am sure that, in the last resort, we achieve far more by gentleness and quietness.

COUNTRY CANVAS

We all enjoy a charming view
Where we can gaze our fill,
And Winter's skilful artistry
Can make it lovelier still.

THE FRIENDSHIP BOOK

OLD Mrs MacAndrew opened her front door to be confronted by two teenagers, a boy and a girl. Now alas, all too often teenagers have a bad name in our society because of the thoughtless behaviour of a few, so Mrs MacAndrew's first reaction was to shut the door firmly in their faces and lock it—but something in their shy smiles stopped her long enough for the girl to say: " Please will you be our Granny?"

" You see," added the boy, " we've started an Adopt a Granny/Grandad scheme at school, and as we know you live alone, Jennie and I chose you."

How glad Mrs MacAndrew was that she hadn't closed that door—those two teenagers became her greatest friends, and every week, in holiday time as well as during term, they called on her, ready and willing to help in any way they could.

Constant days of loneliness were over, and once again she enjoyed baking cakes and pastries—there was now an incentive to do so! What a grand scheme this is, one of mutual benefit, I'm sure.

I SUPPOSE that the best prayers are those that spring spontaneously from our hearts, but sometimes the prayers of others can be of great inspiration to us—probably because it makes us realise that others share our own needs.

A prayer which has helped me, but whose author appears to be unknown is:

> *Lord, temper with tranquillity*
> *My manifold activity,*
> *That I may do my work for Thee*
> *In very great simplicity.*

FRIDAY—FEBRUARY 8.

P LEASE shut the Door "—this brand new notice appeared recently on the door of our local post-office. " I was nearly getting blown away because people *would* leave the door open," the Postmaster told me.

It occurred to me then how important it is sometimes not only that people should shut the door, but also *how* they shut it. When there is a sleeping child, how gently we close the bedroom door. And is there any of us who has not, at some time or other, in a fit of irritation, slammed a door?

But thinking of the Postmaster in his draughty shop as I arrived home after a tiring day, I felt what deep satisfaction there is on these cold winter nights to come home and shut the door on the cold dark world. I don't need a notice to make me do it!

SATURDAY—FEBRUARY 9.

P ROBABLY most of us know the phrase, " the first fine careless rapture," but I wonder how many of us know the source of those familiar words?

They are from a poem by Robert Browning, " Home-thoughts from Abroad ":

That's the wise thrush; he sings each song twice over,
Lest you should think he never could recapture
The first fine careless rapture.

A wise bird. Any joy we have becomes richer and sweeter if we share it with others.

SUNDAY—FEBRUARY 10.

I NTO whatsoever house ye enter, first say, Peace be to this house.

THE FRIENDSHIP BOOK

STELLA COE, who has won world-wide fame as a flower-arranger, lived for many years in Japan. She recalls a beautiful lotus garden where she loved to go " in the peace and quiet of the morning before the hubbub of the day commenced."

She tells how it was said that if one was perfectly quiet and still, one could hear the gentle " plop " when the buds opened in the early morning. She admits, " although I listened intently I never heard this—evidently I was never quiet or still enough! But I *did* have an intense feeling of serenity which I can distinctly recall even after so many, many years."

I think probably all of us could conjure up in our minds some scene of tranquillity we have known—a garden, a forest, a lakeside, a mountain top. To do so is to find an antidote to the rush and strain of life.

THERE was a time when every seaside resort seemed to have its Punch and Judy Show but now these shows are rare events. Recently, however, the Lady of the House and I were invited to a children's party where Punch and Judy were part of the entertainment and we were fascinated to find that the children's enjoyment was as real as we remember it in our own young days.

It reminded me of some words of Dr Thomas Guthrie, the great Scottish scholar, preacher and reformer. In a letter written when he was approaching the end of his life he wrote: " I hope I may ever be child enough to enjoy Punch and Judy, or anything that brings a sunlight smile to children's faces."

Amen to that.

WHEN the concert pianist Harriet Cohen was at the height of her career, she damaged an artery and the nerves in her right hand. That was in 1948. Two years later she made a triumphant reappearance, playing a Concertante for Piano for the Left Hand written especially for her by Arnold Bax.

She continued to nurse her right hand and patiently fought to overcome pain and frustration. At last, in 1952, she was able to play with both hands in a Handel Concerto in the Chelsea Town Hall. For the next eight years she continued to give concerts. Then eye trouble, caused by the strain of practising eight hours a day, often from manuscript, forced her to give up her career.

Harriet Cohen died in 1967. She is still remembered as a great pianist and is written about in many books on the art of piano playing. Many still remember her not only as a great pianist but as a woman of great courage.

ST BASIL, Bishop of Caesarea from 370 to 379 AD, was considered to be one of the greatest early Christian Fathers. He is commemorated by a statue under the dome of St Paul's Cathedral, easily seen from the Whispering Gallery.

It is interesting to note that the statue was one of several placed in the Cathedral about a century ago in an effort made by the then Dean and his colleagues to " cheer up St Paul's ". Why do I find this particularly apt? Because it was St Basil who was responsible for this little gem I came across some time ago: " A good deed is never lost. He who sows courtesy reaps friendship, and he who plants kindness gathers love."

THE FRIENDSHIP BOOK

HAVE you ever heard of " Munsey's Magazine "? Or of Bertha Adams Backus? Probably not, but they are worth remembering if only for a verse the latter published in the magazine as long ago as 1911.

Build for yourself a strong-box,
  Fashion each part with care;
When it's strong as your hands can make it,
  Put all your troubles in there;
Hide there all thought of your failures,
  And each bitter cup that you quaff;
Lock all your heartaches within it,
  Then sit on the lid and laugh.

HARDRAW FORCE in Wensleydale, Yorkshire, must be one of the most spectacular waterfalls in the country—one sheer drop of nearly 100 feet. And the approach to it must be one of the most unusual, too. You can only reach it by going through the Green Lion Inn!

As the Lady of the House and I walked from the Force we heard another visitor say to his friends, " Fancy having all that beauty at your back door!"

Somehow back doors always sound a bit grim, but need they be? Maybe we have at least a strip of garden—or a window box—or a tub of flowers. Maybe we can look up at the sky, and surely sometimes there will be a gleam of sunlight, or indeed even the gleam of a street lamp, or lights at night shining through the coloured curtains of the windows of the houses opposite.

We can't all live with Hardraw Force at the bottom of the garden, but I think we can all have a little beauty at the back door.

THE FRIENDSHIP BOOK

JUDGE not, and ye shall not be judged; condemn not, and ye shall not be condemned: forgive, and ye shall be forgiven.

DR LESLIE WEATHERHEAD, for many years Minister of the City Temple in London, once recalled an occasion in the Blitz when the congregation got drenched. He said: " A fireman fighting the blaze lost control of his hose. It broke the window and soaked half the people listening to my sermon. Those who had come to the service as Congregationalists went out Baptists . . !"

LOOKING round an old church recently the Lady of the House and I noticed how many of the memorials on the wall included the word " benefactor " in their inscriptions.

We tend to think of benefactors as people who give large sums of money to charity or build hospitals or endow scholarships and so on, but there are humbler yet important ways of being benefactors.

Robert Louis Stevenson has an oft-quoted saying about there being " no duty we so underrate as the duty of being happy ", but the end of that passage I think is less familiar. He says, " By being happy we sow anonymous benefits upon the world, which remain unknown even to ourselves, or when they are disclosed surprise nobody so much as the benefactor."

That's a thought! Not just by vast donations, but by our simple happiness we can be numbered among the world's benefactors.

THE FRIENDSHIP BOOK

A DEAR old friend of ours, a gracious lady in her 80's, was at tea with us the other day when suddenly, out of the blue, she said, " My, but our minister has been a great help to me!" Well, he's been a great help to all of us in all kinds of ways, but we wondered just what it was that had made Janet so grateful.

" Well, you see," she said in answer to our query, " the other Sunday he was preaching about prayer, so when he happened to visit me a few days later, I felt I could speak to him of a little problem I have. With my old knees I find it difficult to kneel down and say my prayers at my bedside as I did for years so I say my prayers in bed. But what worried me was that I sometimes fall asleep saying my prayers . . . and it seems such an awful thing to do. But when I told the minister, he just put his hand on my shoulder and said, ' Now, don't you worry about that, Janet. It's better to go to sleep counting your blessings than counting sheep!' "

Whether or not we think of it in terms of prayer, what a good thing it is that our last waking thoughts should be of goodness and beauty, truth and peace . . .

THE novelist E. M. Forster once pointed out that growing old and old age are two quite different things. " Growing old is an emotion which comes over us at almost any age," he said. " I had it myself between the ages of 25 and 30!"

Conversely, someone has said, " Youth is not a time of life but a state of mind." We are indeed as old as we feel. What a pity we so often let ourselves feel we are getting old!

A FRIEND showed me a school magazine with a boy's account of a football match which his team had won by a single goal headed into the net by one of the forwards.

This is how the boy described the incident: " The forwards had tried all ways to score but without result until Jones decided to use his head. It came off first time "!

A FEW of us were talking about moments which stood out in our lives as particularly memorable. Someone spoke of the day he secured his first job, another the day on which he scanned the University Pass Lists and found his name there. Someone else told of the day he was demobbed from the army, and yet another of the moment he was told that his wife was off the danger list after a serious operation.

Then one elderly man who had been listening quietly, said, " My most memorable moment was when I learned that I was a grandfather for the first time and realised that something of myself was going on and on into the unforseeable future."

All grandparents will know exactly how he felt, yet we do not need to be grandparents to have this sense of an influence on the future. All our words and deeds and lives *do* become woven into the pattern of the future. We should never think that we don't count. We *do* . . . and more than we ever realise.

F OR thou wilt light my candle: the Lord my God will enlighten my darkness.

THE FRIENDSHIP BOOK

MY friend Sandy was showing me with great pride some pot-plants in his greenhouse. They were in shapes and colours which I had never seen before.

"They're flowers from the Australian bush," said Sandy. "You saw me planting them. Remember?"

I did. He had emptied the packet of seed on to a fine sieve, lit a bundle of paper on the greenhouse floor and passed the sieve to and fro over the flames. As soon as one or two seeds exploded he put them all into water for a few minutes before sowing.

Sandy explained that some tropical plants produce seeds that can lie dormant for years. Then, when a bush fire comes along, the seeds burst open. When the first rain comes they are ready to rush into life.

As I reflected about this trick of nature, it seemed to me that some of us are rather like these seeds. We just don't know what is in us until a sudden crisis puts us to the test and then we do better than we ever thought possible.

When the road is rough and the wind is blowing
And the going is tough—then the tough get going!

HERE are some brief "Thoughts for the Week" from a church service sheet which a friend sends me from time to time:

"If you can't find a sunny side to life, polish up the dark side."

"The grass may look greener next door, but it's just as hard to cut."

"We see things not as they are but as we are."

"Everything is impossible to the person who doesn't try."

"Think and Thank."

DAYBREAK

For one enchanted moment
  The world seems fresh and new
Before the sunbeams break the spell
  And dry the morning dew.

THE FRIENDSHIP BOOK

L IN YUTANG, the Chinese writer, has contrasted the Western and Chinese attitudes towards the business of growing old. In the West it is faced with reluctance, in China with reverence and eagerness.

There is, he points out, a Chinese god of old age: " High forehead, ruddy face, white beard — and how he smiles!" He gently strokes his flowing beard in peace and contentment, " dignified, because he is surrounded with respect, self-assured, because no-one ever questions his wisdom, kind, because he has seen so much of human sorrow."

That attitude of serenity has something to teach us. So much depends upon our *own* attitude, our own philosophy. Every stage of life brings its own particular blessings—and the Chinese, it is fair to say, hold the young in high regard, too.

Growing old is not a penance or a punishment, not something to hide, but to be welcomed with a cheerful heart.

V ISITORS to Carlisle Castle are sometimes shown a small cell which has one tiny window. Beneath the window are hollows in the sandstone wall. It is said that these are the hand and foot-holds by which, when he was a prisoner there, one of the Macdonald chieftains used to pull himself up and cling to the window ledge to gaze out towards the Border hills and valleys which spoke to him of home. The sight gave him hope and courage.

Whatever our circumstances, there is always a window of hope—though, like that Highland chieftain, we may sometimes have to struggle up to peer through it.

MARCH

FRIDAY—MARCH 1.

JOHN HILLABY, who wrote a fascinating account of his journey on foot from Land's End to John o' Groats, says in one place in his book, " Overhead, the birds sang their heads off. It is unfashionable, I know, to talk about jubilation. Any suggestion that thrushes are glad to be alive on a bright spring morning is romantic old-hat."

He goes on to explain that ornithologists believe that bird-song is strictly purposive. The thrush, for example, is simply trying to lay claim to his territory, saying, " Keep away, keep away! This is mine, this is mine!"

And then John Hillaby adds, " But I must say that on the banks of the Teign that morning, the old notion of creatures being glad to be alive was nicer to think about. And nearer the heart."

I couldn't agree more!

SATURDAY—MARCH 2.

MRS G. HALL of Coppice, Oldham, wrote these lovely lines:

The smallest hint of joys to come can make a sad heart sing, the first small bud upon a tree, a swallow on the wing, the first bright hint of sunlight's gold that seemed so long delayed, heart-warming moments when no one could ever feel dismayed.

The earth may still look bare and cold but when first snowdrops peep, we know that Nature never dies but only lies asleep; eternal life, eternal hope forever shall remain, so long as turning of the year brings springtime's joy again.

THE FRIENDSHIP BOOK

WHEN he saw their faith, he said unto him, Man, thy sins are forgiven thee.

FEW, if any, of us escape moments when we are faced with things we would rather not do—dull, boring, unpleasant tasks. Sir Harold Nicholson had some wise and helpful words to say about such situations:

" I hate drudgery as much as any man, but I have learned that the only way to conquer drudgery is to get through it as neatly, as efficiently as one can. A dull job slackly done becomes twice as dull; whereas a dull job done just as well as you can becomes half as dull."

If you have never thought of it in that way before, I'm sure you'll find it works.

WHEN the gardener of a large estate retired he was asked whether it was the peace of the garden that made him such a contented man.

He replied, " Well, I learn a lot from working in a garden. When people try to quarrel with me, I remember the daffodils in the wind — I know when to bend a little."

It had been a privilege, he said, to have been a gardener and he quoted this inscription from a sundial at Wakehurst Place in Sussex:

Give fools their gold and knaves their power. Let fortune's bubbles rise and fall.

Who sows a field or trains a flower or plants a tree is more than all.

THE FRIENDSHIP BOOK

I MET him only once, but I was most impressed by Sir Robert Birley, who was headmaster of Eton College from 1949 to 1964. He achieved something of a reputation for social reform, delivered the Reith Lectures in 1949, and was a formidable scholar.

But what sticks in my mind is what he said about his own schooldays: " I once came top of a class of 25, and went home elated at having secured first prize. But when my report arrived, it said, ' Bad, but the others were worse '."

A T the end of last century James Aggrey was a young African boy growing up in a Methodist Mission on the Cape Coast. He lived in the missionary's house, helping with the chores, fetching water, and cleaning the missionary's boots.

It soon became clear, however, that he was an extraordinarily gifted young man and before he was 20, he was in a responsible teaching post. Recognising his gifts, the authorities enabled him to go to America for further education and there, before long, he became a professor. Soon, as his fame spread, he preached and lectured across the world.

Years later, he returned to his native Africa and paid a visit to his old missionary mentor. He arrived late at night and there was little chance of talking, but the old missionary waited rather apprehensively for morning, wondering how learning and fame had affected his former pupil.

Next morning he looked out of his bedroom window and there in the yard he saw Aggrey, engaged, as he had been so many years before—in cleaning the missionary's boots!

THE FRIENDSHIP BOOK

THE old Tudor gateway to Ingatestone Hall in Essex is surmounted by a bell turret and a fine French clock. Beneath the clock is written " Sans Dieu Rien "—" Without God Nothing." Every time I see the clock I think of Herbert.

Herbert is a clockmaker in the Yorkshire dales. He lives behind his shop and looks into it through a little window. When the shop door opens, a bell says " Ping " and Herbert pops out like a figure on a Swiss chalet weather guide. When I visit Yorkshire I take my clock repairs to him, and if I have none I still call to see him because he always passes on some words of wisdom.

Herbert thinks men are like clocks. He tells me we should always be going forward, recording all the good hours, and that we shouldn't put time back by dwelling on the unpleasant moments. " Like a clock, it's bad for the works," he says—a timeless truth to be remembered.

I LIKE the story of Dorothy, aged six, who was standing in the bathroom one day when she suddenly asked her mother, " Where does the water come from before it gets into the pipes?"

" From the rivers, dear," Mum replied. " We've got two rivers here, and we get our water from both."

" I see," said Dorothy after a pause. " And which of them is the *hot* river?"

IT is God that girdeth me with strength, and maketh my way perfect.

THE FRIENDSHIP BOOK

GRAHAME GREENE, the novelist, said in a talk on the radio that he became a writer because, as he read the books of Elizabeth Bowen, he was fired to a similar ambition because she wrote with such zest. One could not read her without believing that to write was to live and to enjoy.

Of all the things we can pass on to others and of all the things we can receive from others, I think two of the most valuable are zest and enthusiasm. These, after all, are how most things are communicated from one person to another. We have no longing to do something that we see someone else doing with obvious boredom and reluctance. But enthusiasm is catching! If we really want to get the most out of life then we need to find something we can be enthusiastic about. Life, then, will never be dull.

A CERTAIN father was desperate for a bit of peace and quiet one wet Sunday afternoon, so from his paper's colour supplement he tore out a picture of a map of the world. He got a pair of scissors and cut the map into small pieces and then said to his children, " Come on—put the world together again."

After a bit of grumbling there were a few giggles and whispers, then a period of concentration, at the end of which the youngsters said, " There you are, we've done it."

And so they had—but the picture was not a map of the world. It was a photograph of a very happy-looking family. The children had discovered that was what was on the back of the picture of the map.

And very fitting, too. For isn't the foundation of a united world a happy family?

THE FRIENDSHIP BOOK

SOME years ago, the French entertainer, Marcel Marceau, returned from a round-the-world concert tour to his Paris home. Glad to be home again, he strolled round the grounds of his house and talked to his gardener who had worked there for 25 years and scarcely ever gone outside the district.

He wrote, " I felt he didn't know less about life than I did. He talked so wisely about the things he knew and loved. He was becoming like an old tree himself while I was rushing from one continent to another, so full of impressions that I was like a film half-developed."

Well, I don't know whether the gardener would like being compared to an old tree! But I'm sure we know what Marcel Marceau meant. Valuable as travel may be, we should not underestimate how much wisdom and experience we can gain in what may seem a limited environment, rooted there (like an old tree!) with time to grow, and time to ponder the things about us.

I LIKE a billowy, blowy day
* When the wind goes sweeping by,*
A rollicking, roisterous, roaring day,
* That makes the cobwebs fly.*
A day that takes me off my feet,
* And sets my hat awry,*
The keenest, cleanest kind of day
* With which no others vie.*
Some like balmy, gentle days,
* But those for which I sigh,*
Are the wild and wilful windy days,
* That lift my spirits high.*

ENDURING

Pious builders of our churches
    Raised their towers and steeples high
So that we should be reminded,
    When we look towards the sky,
That they stand, eternal symbols,
While we mortals live and die.

I WONDER if you know the story about the three old monks whose monastery was burned down by an invading army.

The monks escaped and lived in the forest. They found a beautiful glade which they called their cathedral, and there each day they worshipped God. But because their voices were old and cracked the only praise they sang was " The Magnificat ".

They sang this each evening until one day a stranger with a beautiful voice joined them and the old monks stopped singing.

After a while an angel appeared and said: " The Lord wishes to know why there is no praise now sent up to him."

" But there is," said the monks. " Has the Lord not heard this man's beautiful singing—far finer than ours could ever be?"

" Yes," said the angel, " it is beautiful, but that man does not sing to praise the Lord but for the pleasure of hearing his own voice. The Lord wishes *you* to start singing again."

If in life we offer of our best, we need never be ashamed of what we give.

SATURDAY—MARCH 16.

HERE'S a thought for this weekend of Mothering Sunday: " We learn the good things of life at our mother's knee, and the bad things at the other joints "!

SUNDAY—MARCH 17.

WHEN the morning stars sang together, and all the sons of God shouted for joy.

MONDAY—MARCH 18.

SIMNEL CAKES—those rich fruit cakes with thick almond paste—are still a popular delicacy in many places on Mothering Sunday, and round about Easter time.

Probably the name comes from the Latin word *simila,* the fine wheaten flour from which the cakes are made. Still, I like the ancient, though quite unlikely, story that a husband and wife, Simon and Nell, disagreed as to whether the cake ought to be boiled or baked, so they compromised by boiling it first and then baking it, and giving it a combination of their own names!

Unlikely, as I say, yet I can't help feeling that many of our quarrels might be resolved in much the same sort of way.

TUESDAY—MARCH 19.

ABRAHAM LINCOLN once sat down to preside over a historic meeting of his fellow leaders. To their amazement, instead of plunging into the solemn business of the meeting he began to read them an amusing article by the humorist, Artemus Ward. Frequent chuckles interrupted the reading—but they came only from Lincoln. The rest sat stony-faced. It seemed incredible and improper to them to use this serious assembly in such a way.

But Lincoln went on reading, and when he had finished the article he said, " Gentlemen, why don't you laugh? With the fearful strain that is on me night and day, if I did not laugh I should die; and you need this medicine as much as I."

So do we all! Amid the pressures and anxieties of our own life, laughter can provide the safety-valve we all need.

THE FRIENDSHIP BOOK

ON a simple grave in Westminster Abbey is the bare inscription: " THOMAS TELFORD, 1834 "—the simplest of inscriptions befitting a very great but very humble man.

Brilliant engineer of hundreds of miles of roads throughout Britain, builder of canals and bridges including the Caledonian Canal and the famous suspension bridge across the Menai Strait in North Wales, Telford's early work seems far removed from these spectacular achievements.

He began his working life in Scotland as a stonemason's apprentice, engaged mainly in constructing and repairing drystone walls, and even in his later days of public acclaim he always felt great pride in his craft. To the end of his life he kept his stonemason's apron and mallet among his possessions. A great man with a humble heart.

It does us all good sometimes to look back in humility and gratitude to " the rock from which we were hewn, the quarry from which we were dug " and to remember the people and influences which have shaped our lives.

WHEN Pope John Paul II paid a visit to his native Poland in 1979, he met up again with some student friends, who sang away the hours until midnight. One song was " May you live a hundred years ".

At which the Pope asked: " Do you really want the Pope to live a hundred years?"

" Yes!" they exclaimed in unison.

" You'd better let him get some sleep then!" smilingly replied the Pope.

FRIDAY—MARCH 22.

IN one of his books, E. V. Lucas tells the story of Thomas Roberts. As well as being the founder and headmaster of a famous boarding-school he was a renowned map-maker, a distinguished watercolour painter, a skilled woodworker specialising in the making of ships, an expert fisherman, and the inventor of one of the first calculating machines.

This is a fair record of achievement by any standards—but Thomas Roberts had no hands! As a young naval lieutenant he had lost them both in an accident with a grenade. He determined, however, that he would not let his handicap spoil his life. He had equipment made to his own design consisting of wooden blocks attached to his arms with holes to hold his instruments. These he kept in little pockets on his lapels where he could reach them with his teeth.

Don't stories like this make us ashamed of the way we sometimes complain at quite minor hindrances and handicaps?

SATURDAY—MARCH 23.

I WONDER if you saw on television the small boy who had been chosen to press the button detonating the charge that demolished a large block of flats? As the dust settled someone picked him up in their arms and asked, " Were you frightened by that big bang?"

" No," he said.

" Not at all?"

" No," he maintained. " It was quite a quiet bang really!"

I wonder if he was just putting on a brave face? Even if he was, we have something to learn from him. It is not a bad idea to minimise the " bangs of life ".

THE FRIENDSHIP BOOK

KEEP me as the apple of the eye, hide me under the shadow of thy wings.

A MINISTER friend of mine on a preaching visit to a church started his talk to the children brightly by saying, " Does anyone know any Chinese?" To his astonishment two small, very English-looking boys put up their hands. He discovered later that their father worked for a time in China and they had lived there.

However, when he had recovered from his surprise my friend was able to continue his talk which sprang from a book he had read by Wallace Brockway called " Moment of Destiny ". Apparently there is no separate word in Chinese for crisis. Two symbols have to be put together—the one for danger and the one for opportunity.

How much better we would cope with our crises if we saw them also as opportunities to test our courage, action and faith.

IT is a comfort to us lesser mortals to know that sometimes the great and gifted have their lapses. Fritz Kreisler, the violinist, was once playing at a concert with Sergei Rachmaninoff at the piano. Rachmaninoff had the music in front of him but Kreisler was playing from memory. Suddenly, however, his memory failed him, and edging towards the pianist he muttered, " Where are we?"

Rachmaninoff smiled and whispered, " In the Carnegie Hall!"

THE FRIENDSHIP BOOK

THE novelist Compton Mackenzie once said that if he were a godfather wishing a gift upon a child it would be that he should always be more interested in other people than in himself. " That," said Sir Compton, " is a *real* gift."

Even if we have no godfather to bestow this gift upon us it is one we could well seek to cultivate for ourselves. The fact is that everyone—yes, *everyone*—famous or unknown, young or old, good or bad, has something to teach us if we are willing to look and listen. As the Bible says, " No man lives to himself."

SOMEONE has said that one of the most important words in the advertiser's vocabulary after " FREE!" is " NEW!" Newness seems to have an irresistible appeal to many of us. Of course, novelty for novelty's sake can be a snare, but there is a genuine " newness " which *does* lift up our hearts—the " newness " of springtime, for instance, when the earth is clothing itself in the freshness and beauty of new life.

And in the midst of that " newness " in the natural world comes the festival of Easter with its message of the Resurrection and " newness of life ".

Remember, there are Easter carols as well as Christmas carols, and one I specially like is the one by John Mason Neale which begins,

> *The world itself keeps Easter Day,*
> *And Easter larks are singing;*
> *The Easter flowers are blooming gay,*
> *And Easter buds are springing.*
> *Alleluia!*

OASIS

Some spots are meant for loitering,
Letting the world slip by;
Impossible to hurry—
Who would wish to try?

DO you know the story of the king who, in spite of all his wealth and possessions still remained miserable? Seeking the secret of happiness he was told by one of his advisers, " You must find and wear a happy man's shirt."

The king set out on his quest and finally found a tramp singing away happily as he walked along a country road. The trouble was that when the king offered to buy the tramp's shirt he found that the man didn't possess one!

Yes, a poor man can be happy, but no happy man is poor.

SATURDAY—MARCH 30.

MOST of us know that it is in March and October that the clocks are altered in connection with British Summer Time, but some people seem uncertain when they go forward and when they go backward—so we sometimes get people coming to church an hour early or an hour late the following day!

But really, it's quite easy. Remember that Americans call the Autumn " the Fall " and then say, " Spring forward! Fall back!"

Apart from the clocks, it's not a bad motto for life too. There is a time to spring forward with help and sympathy, and a time to fall back in self-denial or modesty. It's important to get them right!

SUNDAY—MARCH 31.

THE Lord rewarded me according to my righteousness: according to the cleanness of my hands hath he recompensed me.

APRIL

MONDAY—APRIL 1.

APRIL 1st—All Fools' Day. Dr F. W. Boreham used to say that it was a pity that the mediaeval jesters—the professional fools—ever went out of fashion. " If now and again," he wrote, " a mediaeval fool—a Wanda or a Touchstone or a Gobbo—could frisk his way, waving his wand and jingling his bells into a Cabinet Meeting, a Synod Hall, an Industrial Tribunal, a Law Court or even a conclave of the League of Nations (as it was then) . . . he would make men see that their pompous wrangling, far from being sublime, is supremely ridiculous."

Another writer, Thomas Carlyle, said that we are mostly fools! April 1st is a good day to examine some of our own follies and foibles and have a good laugh at ourselves!

TUESDAY—APRIL 2.

WHICH was William Wordsworth's favourite flower? Most people would unhesitatingly reply, " The daffodil!" But in spite of his famous poem about the " host of golden daffodils " his favourite was, in fact, a tiny yellow flower called the lesser celandine.

He liked it because it is so common it is rather taken for granted, but especially because it appears in earliest Spring before the trees are in leaf:

Telling tales about the sun,
When we've little warmth, or none.

It's nice to remember that these lowly, humble flowers were loved and celebrated by one of our greatest poets.

A FEW of us were talking together one evening after a meal and the conversation turned to what people call " the rat race " of modern life. One member of the group said rather wistfully, " You know, sometimes I rather envy Robinson Crusoe, alone on his island, away from it all, building his own house, making his own clothes . . ." There another member broke in, " Yes, but you know, even Robinson Crusoe had a wrecked ship to draw on for much of what he had!"

Yes, even Robinson Crusoe was not completely independent. None of us is. Sometimes when we get a bit depressed it is a help to remember how much we owe to others. In all kinds of directions, as Jesus reminds us, " Other men have laboured and we are entered into their labours."

JOHN WESLEY'S rule about wealth which he gave to his followers was, " Earn all you can, save all you can, give all you can." When he was at Oxford he had an income of £30 per year. He lived on £28 and gave the rest away, and so, too, when he received £90 and £120.

The tax man became suspicious and asked for a statement of the silver plate he was sure Wesley must possess. The preacher wrote to the tax office, " I have two silver spoons in Bristol and two in London; this is all the plate I have at present and I shall not buy any more while so many around me lack bread."

The really happy people are those who are more concerned with giving than with getting and having. Wealth is not measured by its amount, but by the good it can do.

THE FRIENDSHIP BOOK

IT is said that when the flag signals first went out reporting the result of the Battle of Waterloo the message began, " Wellington defeated . . ." then mist swirled across obscuring the signal. As the mist cleared the whole message was discernible: " Wellington defeated Napoleon."

So, in the Bible story . . . on Good Friday it must have seemed to many that the message was, " Jesus Christ defeated . . ." Only when the light of Easter dawn broke was the whole message clear, " Jesus Christ defeated sin and death!"

Easter, in the Springtime of the year, marks the victory of good over evil, love over hate, life over death. Hallelujah!

WHEN Sarah Bernhardt, the famous actress, was 71 she had a fall which resulted in having her leg amputated, yet afterwards for a further seven years she toured the world, continuing to delight her audiences.

Her victory over disability was a great tribute to her courage and cheerfulness, but perhaps her secret is best illustrated in an incident as she was wheeled to the operating theatre. To everyone's surprise she started to recite a speech from one of her famous parts. Someone asked if she were doing this to cheer herself up.

" No," she replied, " to cheer up the doctors and nurses. It will be a strain on them."

If someone can think of others in *that* sort of situation, does it not shame and humble us that we are so often wrapped up in self-pity about some of the minor afflictions of our lives?

THE FRIENDSHIP BOOK

JESUS himself stood in the midst of them, and saith unto them, Peace be unto you.

THERE is an incident in " Pilgrim's Progress " when Christian seeks directions from Evangelist. " Do you see yonder wicket gate?" asks Evangelist.

Christian peers into the distance, then shakes his head.

" Do you see yonder shining light?" continues Evangelist.

This time Christian replies, " I think I do."

" Then, go towards the light . . ."

This always reminds me of a hymn we sometimes sing:

I do not ask to see the distant scene, one step enough for me.

There is much to puzzle and perplex us, but if we have some central beliefs and convictions about goodness and truth then they are like lights leading in the right direction.

LOUISA MAY ALCOTT is remembered by most people simply as the author of " Little Women " and similar stories, but she was also a prolific author of inspirational verses. Among them was one she called " My Prayer " in which she asked for the ability—*To smooth the rough and thorny way*
Where other feet begin to tread;
To feed some hungry soul each day
With sympathy's sustaining bread.

What better prayer for us to begin a new day?

QUIET CORNER

WEDNESDAY—APRIL 10.

THE quaintly-named Hall i' th' Wood is an attractive 15th century black and white timbered manor house, near Bolton in Lancashire. Here visitors can see the room where Samuel Crompton invented his famous " spinning mule " which did so much to revolutionise the Lancashire cotton industry.

In the room is a miniature model of the " mule ", but I think the thing which interested me most was a picture of Crompton. The picture is entitled, " Samuel Crompton invents the spinning mule "—and it shows him playing a fiddle!

It is a reminder that we are not wasting time when we are playing an instrument, listening to birdsong or admiring a view. From such moments can come inspiration and enlightenment.

THURSDAY—APRIL 11.

WALKING in the country recently the Lady of the House and I came across a dry-stone dyker repairing some damage and we stopped to chat and to watch him skilfully and firmly replacing the fallen stones.

I was reminded of the story of an old dyker who asked the local minister what the letters D.D. after his name stood for, and was told, " Doctor of Divinity ".

Some time later he had to ask the minister to witness his signature, and he wrote " D.D." after *his* name.

" What does that mean?" asked the minister.

" Dry Dyker," was the reply.

" But you can't put that," said the minister. " It isn't a profession."

" No," replied the old man. " It is an *art,* sir."

THE FRIENDSHIP BOOK

SOME of the writings of the 19th century essayist, poet and philosopher, Ralph Waldo Emerson, are a little difficult to understand, but he could also address himself simply, directly and movingly to ordinary people. Who could take a walk and not feel truly uplifted by these words:

"Never lose an opportunity of seeing anything that is beautiful, for beauty is God's hand-writing—a wayside sacrament. Welcome it in every fair face, in every fair sky, in every fair flower, and thank God for it."

I AM sure I don't know why, but it is said that Sydney Smith, the English clergyman and wit, had four bedrooms, one for each season of the year—Spring, Summer, Autumn and Winter—while Louis XIV had over 400 beds and could have slept in a different one every day of the year and still have a few to spare!

I imagine that most of us are content with one and probably feel like an old friend of mine who used to say, "When I count my blessings I never forget to count my bed among them!" What she really meant, I think, was the blessing of sleep—"Sleep that knits up the ravelled sleeve of care."

I think one of the best things ever written about sleep was in "Don Quixote" by Cervantes: "Blessings on him who invented sleep, the mantle that covers all human thoughts, the food that satisfies hunger, the drink that slakes thirst . . . the balance that equalises the shepherd and the king, the simpleton and the sage."

If we can sleep in peace, blessed indeed are we.

SUNDAY—APRIL 14.

FOR thou hast made him a little lower than the angels, and hast crowned him with glory and honour.

MONDAY—APRIL 15.

MRS HELEN RICHARDS CAMPBELL of Kingston, Ontario, sent me these amusing lines:

Now that I'm over eighty,
I feel I'm not so spry,
For I just like to sit and watch
The turtles—whizzing by!

TUESDAY—APRIL 16.

THEY tell a story in Yorkshire of a country squire and two friends who were discussing which was the best time to cut a length of ash for a walking-stick. The squire maintained that Spring was the best time when the sap was rising because the stick would then be supple. One of his friends disagreed, thinking that Summer when the wood was at the top of its form was the best time. The third man argued that not until Autumn when the wood had matured fully should an ash stick be cut.

The squire said that to settle the argument he would ask his man John who was knowledgeable in every aspect of country life and lore. So he told John about the argument, and then asked him, " Now, can you tell us the best time to cut an ash stick?"

" Yes, surely, master."

" When, then?"

" Why, when you see it!"

How many opportunities we miss because we do not seize them when we see them!

SOME years ago a great exhibition was held in Chicago celebrating " A Century of Progress " in the industrial and scientific world. Over its pavilion, General Motors had inscribed some words of G. K. Chesterton: " The world will never want for wonders—only for wonder."

How easy it is to take for granted not only the wonders of man's achievement but of the natural world in which we live. I don't know who said, " We are only really awake when we wonder," but how right he was. What a wonderful place the world is when we learn to look at it through what Lewis Carroll called a child's " dreaming eyes of wonder ".

THURSDAY—APRIL 18.

IF you live in Liverpool you will have heard of Kitty Wilkinson. In the Lady Chapel of Liverpool Cathedral there is a window dedicated to famous women and Kitty's picture is there, with her work-worn hands for us all to see.

Kitty was a poor, humble woman who lived in a back street of Liverpool. The door of her home was always open to those in need, especially when cholera struck the city. Kitty had a well of clean water and, knowing that dirtiness encouraged the plague, invited neighbours to use her wash-house. She soon realised that more cleanliness in the city was needed and bravely went to the authorities to ask them to provide public baths and wash-houses for the poor.

All because of Kitty Wilkinson, her kindness and her boldness, Liverpool was the first city in the country to have public baths. Kitty has been called " The Saint of the Soap-suds " and the city has never forgotten her.

ANDREW was gazing into the florist's window when I saw him. He was looking less than his usual happy self.

" I've done it again," he said. " Forgotten our wedding anniversary! I had it down in my diary, but I forgot to look—you know how it is."

I knew well enough. Every man knows how it is. He can love his wife with every atom of his being but he can still forget a wedding anniversary.

Every woman, I think, has a calendar built into her brain that tells her when birthdays and anniversaries are due. Men just don't have this gift. So we leave messages lying about the house to remind us. But still we forget and then we're so ashamed that we do exactly what Andrew was doing when I left him. We buy the most outsize bunch of roses we can find and say how sorry we are.

And our wives, being loving, understanding women, forgive us once again!

HAVE you ever noticed that when it is dark, any light, no matter how small, will show up?

In fact, there isn't enough darkness in all the world to quench the light of one small candle, and the late President Sadat of Egypt, one of the outstanding statesmen of recent history, endorsed this when addressing the European Parliament in February 1981.

He said: " I do believe it is better to light a candle than to curse the darkness. I can hear the voice of wisdom saying: ' Light a candle of understanding in thine heart, which shall not be put out.' "

Wise words, which we can all take to heart.

MIRACLE

We bear the gloomy Winter days,
    The cold and damp with fingers numb,
Warming our hearts with promises
    Of better times when Spring will come,
And when we see the bright array
    Of daffodils among the grass,
We know with joyful certainty
    The miracle has come to pass.

E

SUNDAY—APRIL 21.

ALL flesh is grass, and all the goodliness thereof is as the flower of the field.

MONDAY—APRIL 22.

LORD MORAN, who was for many years personal physician to Sir Winston Churchill, was once asked to what he attributed Sir Winston's great age. He replied, " Oh, I think it is 50% nature, 50% me, and 50% Winston." Just as his questioner was obviously about to question his arithmetic, he added with a smile, " I know it adds up to more than 100%—but then Sir Winston is not just one person!"

TUESDAY—APRIL 23.

WHEN John Howard was dying he said: " Give me no monument but lay me quietly in the earth, place a sundial over my grave and let me be forgotten."

But Howard, the pioneer of prison reform, will never be forgotten. His first interest in the miserable plight of prisoners came when he was on a Continental tour. His ship was captured by the French who threw him into prison where he was beaten, starved and neglected.

When he was released he decided to try to do something to help prisoners in England. Appointed High Sheriff of Bedfordshire in 1775, he toured the prisons and was horrified at the conditions of dirt, brutality and darkness. He wrote pamphlets exposing the state of the prisons and eventually Parliament and people began to take notice. So began the reform of the prison system by a man who had experienced their horror for himself.

THE FRIENDSHIP BOOK

JUST time for a quick cuppa, dear," I said to the Lady of the House as I dashed in briefly before setting off again for a meeting.

" It's a good job you don't live in Japan, Francis," she said, smiling. She had just been reading an article about the famous Japanese Tea Drinking Ceremony which is accompanied by lots of ritual—the way the tea is stirred, the cup passed round, and so on—and can last for hours!

I would never have got to my meeting at that rate—or never had my cuppa perhaps. But I did take the point. We *do* tend to rush about too much.

I remember a prayer used by the late Dr W. E. Sangster the well-known Methodist preacher, which contained the words, " Teach me the art of taking minute vacations—of slowing down to look at a flower, to chat to a friend, to pat a dog, to read a few lines of a good book. Slow me down, Lord."

THURSDAY—APRIL 25.

HERE is a verse which was written in my old autograph album many years ago. The words are not unfamiliar but they are especially valuable to me because they were put in my book by an old lady who had been crippled most of her life, and yet she could say,

If any little word of mine
Can make a heart the lighter,
If any little song of mine
Can make a life the brighter,
Lord, let me speak that little word
And take my bit of singing
And drop it in some lonely vale
And set the echoes ringing.

ALL ABOARD!

No-one willingly would spend
Holidays without a friend,
And to have the greatest fun,
Lots are better far than one!
Young and old in different ways
May enjoy their holidays,
But together, it is true,
They can still be happy, too.

THE FRIENDSHIP BOOK

THERE is a story of a Balkan child-princess whose wealthy mother offered her any treat she cared to choose for herself. The child knew that she could ask for the most expensive gifts—and her mother expected her to. Instead, she asked simply to be allowed to go mushrooming the following morning.

At dawn next day the little girl took a basket and ran out excitedly into the field—to see that beside every mushroom a liveried footman had placed a marking flag!

How glad I am not to be that Balkan princess but just an ordinary person whose simple pleasures are never organised out of existence.

YEARS ago in Cheshire a feature of the landscape was the cinder tracks which from time to time were renewed by fresh loads of cinders from the furnaces of the local salt mines. After a new load had been scattered, the road would be very rough and uncomfortable to walk on for a while because no steam rollers were used to level the surface—that job was done simply by countless feet walking along the road.

Someone who remembers those roads recalls a conversation between a father and son whom he happened to be following along one of the tracks.

After emptying his shoes once or twice, the boy said, " Oh, Dad, let's walk on the grassy bank instead."

" No, lad," was the reply. " Better stick to the road. Somebody else will have to tread it down if we don't."

A good philosophy for all of us!

THE FRIENDSHIP BOOK

REJOICE with me; for I have found my sheep which was lost.

YES, it's amazing what you can do if you keep at it," remarked my friend George. Weeks of hard work had turned a piece of waste ground into a delightful and colourful garden.

It reminded me of the story of the Glasgow University lecturer who used to illustrate the effect of small forces on large masses. In his classroom he would have a huge heavy lump of metal weighing as much as a hundredweight suspended from the ceiling. He would then take a basket full of paper pellets, and begin to bombard the heavy iron mass with them. This always caused his students to smile—what did he think he was doing? How could he expect to make any impression on such a heavy object with such tiny light pellets?

At first nothing happened, and the smiles became broader. Then after a time the iron mass would begin to tremble; then it would begin to move; and finally it would swing in a wide arc—all because of repeated blows by little paper pellets.

DURING a period of exceptionally wet weather, an enquirer rang the civic centre in Barnstaple to ask if there were any emergency arrangements in case of floods. The official to whom he spoke replied, " When it comes to floods in North Devon, the Chief Executive is always at the top of the tree."

The best place to be!

MAY

FOR many years Bob Suckling has been a moor-keeper looking after 3000 acres of moorland between Whitby and Guisborough in North Yorkshire. I'm told he knows those acres like the back of his hand. He knows the *sounds* of the moorland, too, and can identify them all—the call of birds, the cry of animals, even the hum of insects.

But, recently he discovered a sound new to him. A television programme was made of Bob and his work, and as he listened he was astounded at the sound of his own voice! " I never thought I sounded like that," he said in his unmistakable North Yorkshire accent. " I can't get over it. Is that really what I sound like?" He had to be assured by his wife, Elizabeth, that it was!

Remember the words of Robert Burns?

O wad some Power the giftie gie us
To see oursels as ithers see us!

THURSDAY—MAY 2.

I THINK the proudest moment of young Johnny's life was when he joined the cubs and appeared in his uniform, eager to carry out his promise to try to do a good deed every day. The opportunity came when he stood at a busy crossroads, and saw an old lady hesitating to cross the street.

Up went Johnny, smartly gave the cub salute, and, taking her by the arm, led her across. How proud he felt until the old lady smiled down at him, " And tell me, how long have you had to wait for someone to take you across the road?"

WANDERING

Just follow the wind if you would stray
Up to the hills and far away.

THE FRIENDSHIP BOOK

WHEN Abraham Lincoln was a young lawyer he was once out riding on horseback with some fellow-lawyers. At one point, on a woodland road, they noticed a baby bird which had fallen from the nest and lay fluttering at the wayside.

After they had gone a short distance Lincoln stopped, turned back and said, " Wait for me. I shan't be a moment."

His friends watched as Lincoln went back to the bird, picked it up, and placed it back on the nest.

" Why did you bother to do that?" asked one of his companions.

" I can only say this," replied Lincoln. " I feel better for doing it. I could not have slept tonight if I had thought that I had left that helpless creature on the road to die."

No wonder he has been called the American Great-heart. All his later great work was shot through with a like compassion.

SATURDAY—MAY 4.

WE all know the old saying that beauty is only skin deep but I found this familiar truth in fresh form in an anonymous verse I came across recently:

Oh, cakes and friends we should choose with care.
Not always the fanciest cake that's there
Is the best to eat! And the plainest friend
Is sometimes the finest one in the end!

SUNDAY—MAY 5.

OUT of the mouth of babes and sucklings thou hast ordained strength.

MONDAY—MAY 6.

THERE are hundreds of people today who look on the motto " Take courage " as their own. Some are little children facing severe physical handicaps; others are older folk exhibiting the courage of perseverance. Charlotte Brontë was advised by no less a person than the poet Robert Southey to give up all idea of becoming an author. She ignored the advice and is now more famous than her critic.

In our own day Alec Guinness, when he was young, was told to give up any idea of becoming a famous actor. His determination and ability have won him fame in the theatre.

These are just two examples of people who won fame through their courage. But the world is packed with ordinary folk who, every day, are facing life's challenges with bravery and stout hearts.

TUESDAY—MAY 7.

A SAINTLY man who was a professor in a scientific department of a university, was once asked by a junior colleague, an agnostic, how he managed to reconcile his religious beliefs with his scientific knowledge. He answered in some words of another scientist, Thomas Edison: " We don't know the millionth part of one per cent about anything. We don't know what water is. We don't know what light is. We don't know what gravitation is. We don't know what heat is. But we do not let our ignorance about these things deprive us of their use."

The implication of the old professor's answer is obvious. There *is* mystery about religion, about God, about prayer, about worship. We can never hope fully to understand such things. Does this weaken our faith? Of course not. We *know* it is true.

THE FRIENDSHIP BOOK

WHEN there are decisions to be made, even small ones, I think it pays to be prudent. In other words, "When in doubt—don't!" But there's an important exception to this rule, and it has to do with simple acts of kindness.

I'm thinking of a rainy day in November last year when a new neighbour of ours had just received some bad news. The Lady of the House, in a moment of impulse, left a friendly note and a small bunch of freesias on her doorstep.

We did not know it until some weeks afterwards, but the gift of those few sweet flowers made the difference between hope and despair for our neighbour. She was given the strength to get through a difficult time, and as a result of that note a warm friendship took root at the same time.

There is no rulebook for compassion. So, when it comes to caring I think you'll agree with my new adage, " When in doubt—do!"

GEORGE BERNARD SHAW once wrote: " When you have toothache, the one happiness you desire is not to have it; when it is gone, you never dream of including its absence in your assets."

That's worth thinking about. When we give thanks it is usually for the blessings we enjoy, for food, for friends, for the beauties of the earth, and so on.

These are life's positive blessings. But we should give thanks, too, for the burdens we *haven't* had to bear, the dangers we have escaped, the pain we have never had to endure. Just now and again, it's worth remembering how lucky we are.

FRIDAY—MAY 10.

WHEN we last visited our old friend Mary she was sitting placidly knitting a garment for one of her grandchildren.

"You enjoy your knitting, Mary, don't you?" said the Lady of the House.

Mary looked up for a moment, then returned to her knitting and said quietly, "I like things that can't be hurried."

Of course, Mary has a lot more time than many of us, but I couldn't help feeling that we might all be a lot happier if we could make more time for some of the things that can't be hurried.

SATURDAY—MAY 11.

ONE of the pioneers of wild-life photography was Oliver G. Pike whose pictures of birds and animals in their natural habitat showed naturalists a great deal they had never understood before.

Ordinary folk, too, were fascinated by his photographs and often wondered how he obtained them. Some people suggested that he disguised himself as a tree or a bush, some that he hypnotised the creatures, and others that he had some strange power over animals, rather like St Francis. Oliver Pike himself said that he had only one very simple secret—patience! He spent hours, days even, waiting in the hide!

To learn patience is to learn one of life's most precious secrets.

SUNDAY—MAY 12.

ASK, and it shall be given you; seek, and ye shall find; knock, and it shall be opened unto you.

ROOFS OF HOME

Nestling in a sheltered nook,
Some houses have a friendly look,
A smiling face that seems to tell
Of happy people there, who dwell
Untouched by modish, modern ways,
Content to pass their peaceful days
With homespun values that have stood
The test of time and still hold good.

ONE day in 1895, widowed Mrs Saunders of Melbourne received a telegram, left at once for China and served there as a missionary until her death 20 years later.

What is so unusual about that? Simply that her two daughters, Nellie and Topsy Saunders, had themselves been missionaries in the Chinese province of Fuh-kien, and the message telegraphed to their mother on that summer's day had told how they had been killed by a gang of rebels.

Their mother's reaction was neither to criticise nor to condemn, but simply to take their place and continue their work.

And work she did, serving the Chinese people with unselfish devotion until she died peacefully in 1915 at the age of 82.

I TOOK our neighbour's little boy to a family service recently. It so happened that at the end of our pew a blind woman sat, with her guide dog in the aisle by her side.

" I didn't know dogs could come to Church," said Garry. I explained that this was a special dog because he was the eyes for Mrs McLean. Garry couldn't take his eyes off the dog, who lay so still and unfidgeting; and then came prayer-time. He pointed to the Guide Dog. " Look, he's saying his prayers, too," he whispered.

I was just about to say that the dog was really having a little nap, when Garry gave me a lovely innocent smile, closed his eyes and bent his head—if the dog could pray, so could he!

I simply bent my head in prayer, too.

THE FRIENDSHIP BOOK

EVERY year thousands of people visit the famous ruins of Fountains Abbey in Yorkshire, but many of them miss what the local people call Surprise View. You take a little path on the hillside with trees and shrubbery thick on either side, then suddenly there is a break and, lying beneath, you see the old abbey, the winding river, the age-old trees.

Whenever I see it I think of the words of a hymn by John Greenleaf Whittier:

> *I know not what the future hath*
> *Of marvel or surprise . . .*

That *is* life — full of surprises.

MARJORIE DUNKELS was driving along one of London's busy streets when her car stalled. Two coloured gentlemen leaped out of the car behind and pushed hers into a side road. A mechanic from a nearby garage got it going again—and refused any payment.

The car stalled again a few miles farther on. A young couple dashed over, threw their shopping bags on to the back seat, and pushed the car up an incline and into a side road once more.

Marjorie continued her journey by taxi—and then, doing some shopping, ran out of cash. A large shop declined to cash her a cheque, but a stranger who had overheard came up and asked how much she wanted. He gave her five pounds in cash, and she gave him a cheque for that amount.

On her return home, Miss Dunkels reflected that the combination of so many unknown Good Samaritans had made her day one to remember gratefully rather than to regret.

LEARNING YOUNG

Even the youngest angler,
When bitten by the craze,
Acquires both skill and cunning,
And, best among his traits,
That useful virtue, patience,
To serve him all his days.

FRIDAY—MAY 17.

OLIVER WENDELL HOLMES, the American writer, once remarked that the human race is divided into two classes: those who go ahead and do something—and those who sit and do nothing and then ask: "Why wasn't it done the other way?"

SATURDAY—MAY 18.

I LIKE the story of the Methodist lay-preacher who arrived at a little country chapel to take a service. As he went in he saw in the porch a collecting box. Thinking it was for the poor, he slipped 50p into it and went on into the vestry. After the service was over one of the office-bearers approached and, after thanking him, said, "You'll understand that we are not able to pay you any fee, but we have a box in the porch so that any who have been helped by the service and feel grateful may put something in, and whatever is found in it we ask the preacher to accept towards his travelling expenses. I am delighted to be able to tell you that today there is 50p. Here it is with our thanks."

The preacher smiled and took it, and went his way. When he got home and was sitting at the table with his wife and children he told them the story and they had a good laugh together. Then the eldest boy remarked, "Well, you know, Dad, if you had put more in, you would have got more out!"

SUNDAY—MAY 19.

THOU shalt love the Lord thy God with all thy heart, and with all thy soul, and with all thy strength and with all thy mind; and thy neighbour as thyself.

F

MONDAY—MAY 20.

A NEIGHBOUR of ours told me that one wet day her small daughter was watching the rain through the window. Suddenly, it stopped raining and the sun came out. All along the centre bar of the window, raindrops hung tremblingly, sparkling in the sun.

The little girl looked at them with delight, and then said, " Oh, Mummy, wouldn't it be lovely if we could string them together into a necklace?"

And wouldn't it be lovely if, more often, we could look at ordinary things through a child's eyes with a child's imagination and sense of wonder?

TUESDAY—MAY 21.

D R STANLEY JONES, for many years a missionary in India, tells of a bird in that country nicknamed " the brain fever bird." He wrote, " In the terribly hot days and nights, when the thermometer rises, its shrill notes rise with it. It cries out, ' Brain-fever, *Brain-fever,* BRAIN-FEVER!' It is enough to drive one mad to listen to it. It was on the point of getting on my nerves one day when I overcame it for ever by making it sing a new song, for I interpreted its notes as " Hallelujah, *Hallelujah,* HALLELUJAH!' "

There are lots of noises which are apt to get on our nerves and, at night, disturb our sleep. I believe they can often be transformed for us if we give them a different interpretation. I remember once at camp being kept awake by a companion's rhythmic snoring until I transformed the sound for myself into the ebbing and flowing of the waves on the sea-shore—and I was soon asleep.

Why don't you try it!

THE FRIENDSHIP BOOK

S MITH of Smiths " was the name given to the celebrated clergyman-author, the Rev. Sydney Smith. He spent a long ministry in Yorkshire as well as London and Bristol and was a great believer in dishing out advice. Some of it was amusing, but sound. When life brought its drawbacks or things were difficult he had lots of rules to help keep up his spirits. These included the following:

" Take short views of human life, not further than dinner or tea."

" Be as busy as you can."

" See as much as you can of those friends who respect and like you and of those acquaintances who amuse you."

" Don't expect too much of human life—a sorry business at the best."

" Don't be too severe on yourself or underrate yourself, but do yourself justice."

" Be firm and constant in the exercise of rational religion."

T HE well-known singer, Johnny Mathis, asked in a TV interview about his background, said, " Coming from a poor family, as I did — well, no, not really a poor family. We just didn't have any money!"

It was said half-humorously, but as the singer went on to explain, his home was rich in many other things — family loyalty and solidarity, happiness, culture, music and much besides. Of course, money and material things have a necessary place in our lives but don't let's forget the uncounted (and often uncountable) wealth which all of us possess if only we will look for it.

FRIDAY—MAY 24.

HAVE you come across this rather different definition of " Poise "? " Poise is the art of getting results by raising the eyebrows instead of the roof."

SATURDAY—MAY 25.

STEPHEN was a shy, withdrawn boy of 11, who never joined in anything, but much preferred to sit by himself. He attended a special school in Paris organised by Madame Dorothea, an Englishwoman.

One evening she read out to him a piece of poetry by another Stephen—Stephen Spender. She read of " corridors of light where hours are suns endless and singing . . . "

The youngster didn't say anything, but next morning Madame Dorothea was awakened at sunrise by the rattle of the lawnmower beneath her bedroom window. She looked out, meaning to protest at the disturbance, but the words died on her lips. The rising sun sent splendour tumbling down the wet paths which young Stephen had cut in the lawn.

" Look," he called out proudly. " I'm making corridors of light!"

That was the turning-point. Young Stephen has now passed through college and university, his abilities released by the power and inspiration of a piece of poetry.

SUNDAY—MAY 26.

HE shall feed his flock like a shepherd: he shall gather the lambs with his arm, and carry them in his bosom and shall gently lead those that are with young.

Monday—May 27.

WHEN Charles Waterton was a schoolboy away back in the 1790's he was once stopped by a poor woman asking for alms. " But I have nothing," he said, and then hesitated, " nothing but this," and he felt behind the hem of his jacket and gave her a needle!

What the woman thought we do not know—but it was certainly a greater gift than she realised. Already Charles Waterton was passionately interested in birds and animals—an interest which in later life was to make him a great naturalist. That needle was valuable to him for blowing birds' eggs, but he gave it away.

No wonder that, as well as achieving fame in his profession, he was also to be greatly loved for his charity and generosity to all kinds of causes. Giving was in his heart.

Tuesday—May 28.

HERE is a verse from Phyllis Birchall which will strike a chord in most hearts:

A wedding anniversary is such a special date,
A day to be remembered and a day to celebrate,
A day to thank each other for the joys you both have known,
For friends and for the kindness that many folk have shown,
A day to offer up a prayer of thanks to God above,
For all the blessings of this life, and his unfailing love,
And when the day has ended, and there's time to meditate,
Remember the vows you both exchanged on this anniversary date.

GRANDEUR

At times we can but stand and gaze
In awe at Nature's majesty.
So it has been since earliest days
And to the end of time·will be.

THE FRIENDSHIP BOOK

THE Lady of the House has always admired people who can draw, and when a neighbour suggested she should join an Art Group which he was organising, she decided to go along.

Now I am enjoying the benefit of the lessons she is receiving.

"The first thing, Francis, is to forget what you know. You know a chair has four legs the same size. But that's not what you see when you look at the chair. If you drew the legs all the same size you would never be able to draw a chair that looks like what you see. You understand?"

I do—I suppose. But one thing for sure, since the Lady of the House started going to her class, I've been looking at everything around me in a way I never did before.

Try drawing a chair and you'll see what I mean!

GEORGINA HALL of Oldham, Lancashire, often sends me a verse or two. This one reached me the other day and I have cut it out and pasted it in my scrapbook:

If you have family, home and friends,
You've wealth on which all life depends.
So say a prayer of thanks each day
For all the joys that come your way.

THOSE of us who find it helpful to begin and end the day with prayer know exactly what Mahatma Gandhi meant when he said, "Prayer is the key of the morning and the bolt of the evening."

JUNE

SATURDAY—JUNE 1.

MARY CRAIG was one of those courageous mothers with a mentally-handicapped son. When another son was born to her she was dismayed to find that he, too, had a mental handicap. Many of her friends felt for her deeply. One of them cried for two whole days; she wanted to write to Mary but couldn't bring herself to do it.

Mary was disappointed that her friend had apparently not cared enough to write, and when they next met she said so, somewhat bluntly.

Later, her friend told her that ever since then, she had written immediately to anyone she knew to be in any kind of trouble.

Mary had learned a lesson, too—that silence from a friend does not always mean indifference; while her friend had realised that people with a special problem need to know that other people care. Our love, our sympathy and our prayers can mean so much to others at a crisis point in life.

SUNDAY—JUNE 2.

AND he sent his twelve disciples to preach the kingdom of God, and to heal the sick.

MONDAY—JUNE 3.

I HAVE come across many definitions of friendship but I specially like the anonymous French saying which, when translated, reads, " Love is blind; friendship closes its eyes." Who among us is not grateful for friends who close their eyes to our faults?

THE FRIENDSHIP BOOK

I WONDER how many of my readers will recognise their own larder in these lines by Miriam Eker:

The sugar's in the caddy
  That's plainly meant for tea —
The coffee's in another tin,
  Where salt should surely be!
The custard, you'll discover,
  Will bear the label " Rice " —
And if you want the barley,
  It's sure to be in " Spice ".
And yet, in all this chaos,
  Is it instinct, or a fluke?
My wife is never at a loss,
  She knows just where to look!

AT the beginning of the 16th century, a humble man and his wife lived in the village of Gifford, in East Lothian.

They did not have many worldly goods, but had what they considered something better. They were " rich towards God ", and determined to give their child a better education than they had had.

They toiled and pinched, and sent their boy first to Haddington Grammar School, and then to the University of Glasgow, thus giving him the basic equipment for life.

That lad—his name was John Knox—became the leader of the Scottish Reformation. A man of God, who was not only a powerful preacher, but an advocate of sound education.

We do not know the names of his parents, but the greatness of John Knox was due in no small measure to their labour and sacrifice.

HOW long will you be away, Mary?" I asked our old friend, as she prepared to go on holiday.

" Oh, I'll only be away for a week," she replied, and then added with a smile, " But really, Francis, my holiday will go on for *months* afterwards—every time I think about it!"

It reminded me of someone who said, " The time to enjoy a holiday is about three weeks after unpacking!" If a holiday—or any other good thing—doesn't remain with us long after it has happened then we have missed part of its real benefit.

THAT talented poetess, Georgina Hall, sent me these lovely lines which she calls " Retreat ":

It may be old and tumbledown from a stranger's point of view,
It may not boast of anything that's modern, smart or new,
It may not bring the leisure that a house in town might bring,
But I can boast of sights and sounds to make a sad heart sing.
I have an old world garden filled with million scents divine,
The treasured gift of God's clean air, the silver stars a-shine,
A spreading oak upon my lawn by age endowed with grace,
And green hills all around me with their far-off pleasant face.
I bless the hand that led me to this sanctuary of rest;
Of all God's gifts to me I count my home the very best.

SATURDAY—JUNE 8.

A FEW of us were talking together recently about sermons and one of our number told a story which was new to me. It was a comment about the length of the sermons of the two preachers in a certain church. A member of the congregation had been heard to say: " I prefer the curate's sermons because he says, ' Finally . . .' and finishes, but the vicar says, ' Lastly . . .' and lasts!"

SUNDAY—JUNE 9.

A ND as ye would that men should do to you, do ye also to them likewise.

MONDAY—JUNE 10.

T HE railway carriage was crowded, hot and stuffy but all the passengers were bearing it patiently except one irritable man who complained about the heat, the dirty carriage, the fact that the train was running late, and that children were running up and down the corridor.

There was an almost audible sigh of relief when the train slowed down at a station and he prepared to leave, causing a good deal of disruption as he gathered his things together. Just before he stepped out onto the platform he turned back and asked curtly, " I haven't left anything behind, have I ?"

The other passengers shook their heads silently, and he departed.

" You know he *has* left something behind," said one of the passengers.

" He has ?" queried another.

" Yes," was the reply. " A thoroughly bad impression!"

THE famous tenor, Enrico Caruso, was once asked what it was that made a great singer. He is reputed to have replied, " A big chest, a big mouth, 90% memory, 10% intelligence, lots of hard work, and something in the heart."

How seriously he meant some of those things I am not sure, but how important is that last thing he mentioned—to have " something in the heart ". We may have all sorts of skills and accomplishments, or we may just be very ordinary people, but for all of us it is the gentle, loving touch in the heart that makes all the difference.

WE have a friend who, when he is offered something he hasn't tasted before—some food or drink—will say, more than half-seriously, " No, thank you. I don't like it—because I've never had it."

Not the best of reasons!

I was reminded of this when I read some words of the late Joyce Grenfell: " One form of holiday I swore I would never take is a cruise. The idea of being trapped at sea with a crowd of people bent on killing time, dressing up for gala evenings, and feeling compelled to be a joiner whether one wishes or not—none of it is for me."

But in fact, some friends invited Joyce and her husband to join them, and made it sound so attractive that they consented—and found it one of the best holidays they had ever had!

I am sure there are lots of things we say we don't like—just because we've never done them. There is a lot to be said for going to fresh places, meeting new people, doing things we've never done before. Try it!

THANKS

Home with their harvest from the sea
They throng the harbour once again.
Can we forget the lifelong debt
We owe this hardy breed of men?

THURSDAY—JUNE 13.

I'M feeling blue." " I'm in the pink!" " She's green with envy." " He went as red as a beetroot." How expressive colours seem to be of feelings and emotions!

Moreover, psychologists tell us that colours can have a great effect on the way we act. One well-known football trainer won't allow his players to wear dull-coloured track suits. Bright colours, he says, greatly increase energy.

Well, I wouldn't know about that, but I know that when the Lady of the House puts a vase of brightly-coloured flowers on the table it does seem to cheer me up. So do the new bright curtains she chose for my study.

You know, I have heard people choose dark-coloured fabrics because they say, " They won't show the dirt so quickly." What false economy! We can't bring too much colour into our lives—and into other people's.

FRIDAY—JUNE 14.

JOHN RUSKIN, the 19th century critic, wrote about art, literature and music and had wise things to say about them all.

Of music, he wrote, in answer to a child's question, " There's no music in ' a rest ', Katie, that I know of: but there's the making of music in it. And people are always missing that part of the life-melody."

Perhaps it sounds a bit like a sermon, but how true it is that much of the discordance of life's " melody " is due to our lack of quiet places, quiet times and quiet thought. They *do* help the music of life.

SATURDAY—JUNE 15.

HERE is a verse dedicated to all fathers, written by Miriam Eker:

> *A little face that's held aloft*
> *For Daddy's farewell kiss,*
> *An early morning ritual*
> *That no-one likes to miss.*
> *A little hand that waves and waves,*
> *As Daddy goes his way,*
> *A little heart that's full of woe,*
> *That Daddy cannot stay.*
> *A little face, when evening comes,*
> *That's squashed against the pane—*
> *A little heart that's so content,*
> *For Daddy's home again!*

SUNDAY—JUNE 16.

IF a son shall ask bread of any of you that is a father, will he give him a stone? Or if he ask a fish, will he for a fish give him a serpent?

MONDAY—JUNE 17.

THE Catholic hymn-writer F.W. Faber used to stress the importance of saintliness in everyday life. His hymns, such as " Souls of men, why will ye scatter?" and " My God, how wonderful Thou art," are well known, but here is something he once wrote in prose:

" Remember that the opportunity for *great* deeds may never come, but the opportunity for *good* deeds is renewed day by day. The thing for us to long for is the goodness, not the glory."

Well, here is another day—and another opportunity.

GIPSY SMITH, the great evangelist of a past generation, was once approached by a phrenologist who proceeded to " feel his bumps."

" What are you doing?" asked Gipsy Smith.

" I am trying to find the secret of your success," said the man.

" Then you are feeling too high," said the evangelist. " The secret lies not in the head but in the heart."

This is not, of course, to discredit the power of the mind and the place of thought. Much of what is best in what we call progress has come to us when men and women have dedicated their minds to making the world a better and happier place. Yet most of us have to admit that *our* particular contribution to the life of the world is not in the realm of intellect, but of love, of compassion, of caring.

Gipsy Smith was not a man of great learning — but a man with a great heart. With the key of love we, too, can unlock doors that would never yield to mind alone.

WEDNESDAY—JUNE 19.

RACHEL FIELD, the American poet and writer, wrote a little verse which reminds us how even the most ordinary things in life can be exciting if we determine to view them so.

She writes:

> *Doorbells are like a magic game,*
>   *Or the bran-tub at the fair—*
> *You never know when you hear one ring*
>   *Who may be waiting there.*

Life can never be boring to someone who is always awaiting its surprises.

I DON'T know what he sees in her!" I once heard a woman say of the girl her son was courting. " It must be true that love is blind." Thinking about it afterwards I remembered that a wise man once said, " Love is NOT blind. It sees more, not less. And because it sees more, it is willing to see less."

Yes, love sees with the inward eye, and although it is aware that the faults and failings are there, yet because it sees, *with love*, those same faults and failings are not nearly so important as they appear to others.

IN some fairgrounds there is an amusement known as a Mirror Maze. To add to the confusion of any kind of maze is the fact that whichever way you look you can see nothing and no-one but yourself!

Some people, of course, do not need a mirror maze to achieve this effect! Mrs Dale Carnegie tells of a widow she tried to help to " build a new life, a new form of happiness from the ashes of the old." The woman would have none of it. " No," she replied firmly. " I don't believe I will ever really be happy again. I'm not a young woman any more. My children are all grown up and married and there will be no place for me."

She was in a mirror maze of her own making! Just count up the number of times she uses the word " I ", " me " and " my ". Her thoughts are turned inward upon herself. Her family, friends, some useful piece of work, the needs of the community in which she lived, all these seemed not to figure in her thoughts at all. Yet for her—and for all of us—that can be the way out of the mirror maze of self-pity.

G

SATURDAY—JUNE 22.

YEARS ago in a little Yorkshire village there lived a vicar who loved to walk in the solitude of the countryside. To reach it, however, he had to walk through the village and time and again he would be stopped by members of his flock who wanted to chat to him. By the time they had finished with him it was often too late for his walk.

At last he found a way to avoid them. He built some stepping stones across the stream behind his vicarage so that he could slip out of the back door, cross the stones, and reach the open fields without meeting any one. These "hipping stones", as Yorkshire folk call them, were his escape route.

Sometimes, amid the business of all our lives we all need "hipping stones", our retreat into silence and solitude. Like the vicar we may find it in the countryside, or it may be in music, in an engrossing book, the silence of an ancient church, or simply the peace of our own room. "Hipping stones" can help us to slip away for a little from the pressures of daily life so that we can come back refreshed and ready once again for the fray.

SUNDAY—JUNE 23.

LOVE your enemies, do good to them which hate you.

MONDAY—JUNE 24.

THE local grocer's shop-window was full of stickers advertising special offers to lure customers. Among the stickers was a picture of a smiling face with this advice: " A cheerful smile is the best sauce for breakfast."—And it costs nothing!

A FRIEND sent me this cutting from his local church magazine:

" *IN MEMORIAM:* We were saddened to hear recently of the unexpected death of one of our most active members, Someone Else. Someone Else's passing creates a vacancy which will be difficult to fill. Whenever leadership was mentioned, this wonderful person was looked to for inspiration as well as results. ' Someone Else ' we would say, ' can work with that group.' When there was a job to do, a meeting to attend or a class to teach, we all knew that Someone Else would do it.

" It was common knowledge that Someone Else was among the largest givers in the parish. Whenever there was a financial need, everyone assumed that Someone Else would make up the difference.

" Someone Else was a wonderful person, often appearing to be superhuman. But a person can only do so much. Were the truth known, everybody expected too much of Someone Else. Now Someone Else is gone. Who is going to do the things we were too willing to let Someone Else do?"

I'VE just come across a little saying by a writer called Charles Beard. It's so very simple, yet conveys the profound truth that when things are at their blackest you often see some shining and hopeful thing—the kind action of a friend or neighbour, for example—which otherwise you would never have discovered. Here it is:

" *When it is dark enough, you can see the stars.*"

I like it. I might even have it framed to hang on my wall.

REAL WEALTH

Those who share in Summer's bounty,
Living close to Nature's beauty,
Need not travel far to find
Riches for the heart and mind.

THURSDAY—JUNE 27.

SOME time ago, a Japanese delegation visiting Israel said they would like to lay a wreath on the tomb of the Unknown Soldier.

Israel, however, does not have a tomb so precisely inscribed, so Premier Golda Meir directed that the wreath should be laid on the most impressive tomb in evidence, which happened to be that of Mendelssohn.

One of the Japanese Embassy staff who could read the Hebrew inscription pointed out that this was not the Unknown Soldier's tomb, but that of the composer.

Mrs Meir was completely unperturbed. " That is perfectly true," she replied quickly. " Mendelssohn was a very great composer—but as a *soldier* he was absolutely unknown."

FRIDAY—JUNE 28.

AILEEN E. PASSMORE wrote many lovely verses. This is one of my favourites. It's called " Little Things."

Give me the little homely things:
A hob whereon a kettle sings,
A kitchen floor of cheerful tiles,
The smell of ironing, children's smiles,
Roast chestnuts on a winter day,
A bed with quilt of patchwork gay,
A morning spent with spade and trowel,
Cold water and a clean white towel,
A firelit room, the caw of rooks
Amid the treetops, friendly books,
A bowl of wallflowers in the sun,
An easy-chair when work is done—
Thank God for all the joy that springs
From life's most precious " little things "!

THE FRIENDSHIP BOOK

THE famous author and journalist, G. K. Chesterton once wrote, "The really great man is the man who makes every man feel great."

He was "great" in almost every sense of the word. Big in stature and big in outlook. On another occasion he declared: "I always enjoy myself more than most. There's such a lot of me having a good time."

A writer with a far different outlook was Thomas Carlyle, the historian who once wrote: "All greatness is unconscious, or it is little and naught."

A much earlier, and almost forgotten pagan writer, Mencius, who lived from 372 to 289 BC, wrote: "The great man does not think beforehand of his words that they may be sincere nor his actions that they may be resolute—he simply speaks and does what is right. The great man is he who does not lose his child's heart."

Aristotle, the Greek philosopher, believed: "To enjoy the things we ought, and to hate the things we ought has the greatest bearing on excellence of character."

While Miguel de Cervantes, the 16th century Spanish author who wrote "Don Quixote", had a similar idea that greatness arose from the person being unaware he was great. Obviously greatness did not always mean fame to him, for one of his definitions applies to many ordinary people: "Great people," he said, "are able to do great kindnesses."

WHOSOEVER shall receive me receiveth him that sent me: for he that is least among you all, the same shall be great.

 JULY

MONDAY—JULY 1.

IN his book, " Be Happier, Be Healthier ", Gaylord Hauser tells how, trying to get to sleep in a hotel in the centre of a noisy city, he mixed himself a kind of " mental sleeping draught ".

He wrote, " For sound I took the soothing theme of the lullaby from the light opera *Erminie* which I have always loved. For sight I went in memory to my home in New York and from the wall took a Renoir picture of a peaceful old man sitting outside a rural inn door. For taste I used the remembrance of tree-ripe peaches as I had eaten them a few weeks ago. For odour I added a little gardenia from a California garden. And for touch, the remembrance of the cool, refreshing waters in which I had swum just two days ago—the waters of the Mediterranean."

We all have our own memories of peace and beauty, of fragrance and delight. How delicious they are!

TUESDAY—JULY 2.

THERE was a time when I thought that the Wayside Pulpit method of church publicity was falling into disuse, but I have recently noticed more and more churches using this method of speaking to the passer-by. Here are a few examples I have collected over the past few weeks:

You can't keep a chip on your shoulder when you are bowed in prayer.

Like a piano, you may not be grand but you can be upright.

Good arithmetic: Happiness adds and multiplies as we divide it with others.

THE FRIENDSHIP BOOK

ONCE when T. H. Huxley was walking on a Scottish moor he plucked up a moss-cup and stood examining it through his pocket magnifying glass. A shepherd nearby watched him curiously and when Huxley saw him he asked if he would like to look at the flower through the glass.

The shepherd took it and gazed in wonder through the lens. Then, after a long pause, he said, " Sir, I wish you had never shown it to me."

" Why?" asked Huxley in surprise.

" Because," the shepherd replied, " I tread on thousands of them every day of my life."

Well, of course, that kind of treading is impossible to avoid, but we do well to be sensitive about " treading on people's feelings ", upon their hopes and enthusiasms. Remember what W. B. Yeats wrote:

I being poor, have only my dreams . . .
Tread softly because you tread on my dreams.

I LOVED the story of two American visitors to an Oxford college where Mahatma Gandhi once stayed.

The visitors revered his memory and were excited to think that they were sleeping in the very room which Gandhi had used. However, there were two beds, and they did not know which was the right one. So they set the alarm for the middle of the night, and when it rang, they changed beds, so that each of the them could be sure of having occupied the bed in which the Mahatma had slept. Next morning they told the College Warden what they had done.

He smiled as he said: " Ah, but when Gandhi slept here, he slept on the floor!"

THE FRIENDSHIP BOOK

IT is said that the playwright George Bernard Shaw once remarked: " People who can't do anything, criticise those who can." Fortunately there have always been some whose motto has been, " If you can't do — encourage."

Many famous men and women owe their success to encouragement. Often it has been given by people who, although they could not themselves accomplish great things, knew the value of a potential winner and gave every encouragement to boys and girls, men and women.

Edward Garrett, a publisher's reader, was one of Britain's great encouragers. Although his own writing was not as successful as he sometimes wished, he was always quick to recognise and encourage talent in others. Such authors as John Galsworthy, H. E. Bates, H. G. Wells, Joseph Conrad, W. H. Davies and Edward Thomas all owed much to his help during their early careers.

If in our own simple way, we can encourage others — well there is no knowing where that encouragement may lead!

THE late Will Rogers, the American comedian, brought laughter to thousands, but he also had a very serious side to his nature. In an address given in the Tremont Temple, Boston, he once said, " I never met a man I didn't like."

That doesn't tell us much about the people he met because they can't *all* have been nice, but it does tell us a great deal about Will Rogers himself.

When we look for the best in people there really are a lot of likeable folk about!

H

THE FRIENDSHIP BOOK

HE that is not with me is against me: and he that gathereth not with me scattereth.

THIS verse has one atrocious rhyme, but I like it for what it says:

" Popping in " or " down " or " round "—
Of course it just means walking.
But hasn't it a homely sound
When you hear two neighbours talking—
For every housewife knows—or oughter—
That " popping " makes each street the shorter!
See what I mean?

WE all know what a heartening thing loving kindness can be. Nor is it something that can be imitated — the genuine thing shows up the false just as gilt is shown up by real gold.

Some of our greatest men and women have possessed this gift. Edith Cavell, shot by the Germans during the First World War, is remembered in her native village of Swardeston, Norfolk, not so much for her valour and heroism, as for her loving kindness displayed in so many ways to her father's parishioners and to the children she taught in Sunday School. Many of these are very old people now, others are dead, but their families remember her sweetness and prove the truth of William Wordsworth's lines that:

. . . the best part of a good man's life
His little nameless unremembered acts of kindness
and love.

THE FRIENDSHIP BOOK

THE Lady of the House came in smiling broadly the other day. " I have just given little Jenny next door a bit of my home-made toffee and she said, ' Oh, thank you ever so much, Mrs Gay. Would you like a ride on my bicycle?' "

Maybe the Lady of the House was smiling at the thought of herself on Jenny's tiny bicycle, but I rather think she was smiling too because of the happy appreciation received from a small child for the simplest act.

The writer John Ruskin once said, " Give a little love to a child and you get a great deal back."

A FRIEND of ours lives in a house with a rather drab outlook, facing on to the brick wall of a neighbouring building. However, on the bar across the middle of the window inside she has placed a number of coloured glass bottles of different shapes and sizes. When the sun shines through them it brings a wonderful brightness into her room, and even on a dull day there usually seems enough light to give a pleasant, colourful glow about the window.

This set me thinking as to whether we might not all bring a little more colour into our lives—a vase of flowers, a brightly-coloured picture, a few brilliant cushions scattered about the room. And what about the kitchen? Even pots and pans give scope for colour. Then, on a dull, rainy day what cheer we might bring to others as well as ourselves by wearing a brightly-coloured mackintosh and carrying a gay umbrella.

Yes, colour is a wonderful thing. I don't think we can have too much of it!

THE FRIENDSHIP BOOK

I WAS interested to see in a church magazine recently that the once popular feature of church life, the Faith Tea, still has its place in some of our churches. There are those who think that this bringing and sharing of food for a communal meal goes right back to the Love Feasts of the early church.

Of course, the Love Feast, or the Faith Tea, does depend on people's willingness to bring and share with others. I heard of a minister who was appealing for gifts of food for a Faith Tea in his church and he said, "What we want is not abstract promises, but concrete cakes!"

Not only in Faith Teas, but in all kinds of situations it is easier to make promises than to keep them. Not just saying but doing, not just promising but fulfilling is the important thing. For us to keep our word, and to be known as people who keep their word, is more than wisdom and riches.

PASTOR MARTIN NIEMOLLER earned a reputation for standing up to the Nazis. I was very struck by his reflections on what happened:

"First they came for the Jews, and I did not speak out—because I was not a Jew. Then they came for the communists, and I did not speak out—because I was not a communist. Then they came for the trade unionists, and I did not speak out—because I was not a trade unionist. Then they came for me—and there was no one left to speak out for me."

He never forgave himself for his silence when he should have raised his voice—but he made up for it nobly later on.

FOR every tree is known by his own fruit. For of thorns men do not gather figs, nor of a bramble bush gather they grapes.

MONDAY—JULY 15.

VISITORS to the lovely Swaledale village of Muker, North Yorkshire, may pause outside the little stone-built school to read the memorial plaque to two of Britain's most famous naturalists and photographers, Richard and Cherry Kearton.

They were born towards the end of last century at Thwaite, a hamlet near Muker. Each day they had to walk to and from school, carrying their lunches. No school buses or dinners in those days!

It was on their daily walks that the two boys first began taking an interest in wild animals, birds, flowers and the seasonal changes.

Neither of them forgot their boyhood environment and even when they became famous, they often visited Swaledale. Richard once observed, " My fellow Dalesfolk are a shrewd, hard-headed lot, slow to take strangers into their confidence, but true as steel in any friendship established upon mutual goodwill and understanding."

That still applies to Dalesfolk. And to a certain extent the goodwill and understanding also applies to any friendship, too.

TUESDAY—JULY 16.

I LIKE this anonymous Beatitude which I came across the other day: " Blessed is the man who is too busy to worry in the daytime—and too sleepy to worry at night."

CAREFREE

Holidays are happy days,
     But they can mean much more—
Heaping up rich memories
     To swell our lifetime's store.

THE FRIENDSHIP BOOK

THE writer, Rita Snowden, once reflected that it's not always the most deserving people who have memorials erected in their memory. She said: " So many of the people who most deserve them never get them. There should be one for the man who taught us to drink tea—what would life be without tea?—and a colourful one for the man who first combined strawberries and cream. We should keep before us the immortal memory of the inventor of stainless cutlery who delivered us from the drudgery of knife-cleaning. And there should be a memorial to the inventor of the modern shop window for all the pleasure it has given us."

I am sure we could all make out a list of the people we think ought to have memorials. It would perhaps make us a little more grateful for what we sometimes call the " common mercies of life " and help us to realise how much we owe to others.

EIGHTY years or so ago, an American magazine held a competition for the best definition of " Success ". The winner was a lady named Bessie Anderson Stanley, and this was her definition:

" He has achieved success who lived well, laughed often, loved much. Who has won the respect of good women and the love of little children. Who has filled his niche in life and accomplished his task. Who has left the world a better place than he found it, whether by a song, a poem or an improved flower. Who has looked only for the best in others and given the best he had. Whose life was a dedication, whose memory a benediction. This constitutes success."

And who's to say she wasn't right?

WHEN the Lady of the House returned from a meeting the other day she told me how the speaker had, at one point, caused unexpected and unintended laughter by saying, " One fine day recently my wife and I thought we would go for a walk in the country, so we got in the car . . .!"

Well, it sounds a contradiction, yet the car probably took them to a part of the country which they couldn't have reached *just* by walking.

It is easy to be a bit scornful of people who " go for a walk in the car ", yet how many of our natural abilities are helped and enhanced by what we may call " artificial aids ". Spectacles, hearing aids, walking sticks and the like help our physical infirmities. Labour-saving devices of one sort or another take drudgery out of many chores. Books, wireless and television have done much to widen our horizons. And so we might go on and on—all " artificial " things, yet if they enrich our life, let's be truly grateful for them.

BROWSING through some magazines nearly one hundred years old, I came across this verse about friendship—just as meaningful today as it was then:

The longest day is in June, they say,
The shortest in December.
They did not come to me that way:
The shortest I remember—
You came a day with me to stay
And filled my heart with laughter;
The longest day—you were away—
The very next day after.

THE FRIENDSHIP BOOK

LOOK upon mine affliction and my pain; and forgive all my sins.

NOTHING is truer than the common observation that we all make mistakes. The important thing is not to let our mistakes get out of proportion and give us a sense of failure. That's why I like this little saying of Thomas Fuller: " Every slip is not a fall."

All right. We've slipped up—and it's a pity. But it's not a disaster. Let's keep on going, encouraged by the thought that it could have been so much worse.

THE Lady of the House and I set off into the country with our sandwiches and flasks, and as we sat on the grass enjoying our picnic I remembered, as I always seem to on these occasions, the story in St. Mark's Gospel where the multitude of 5000 " sat down on the green grass ".

What a pity we tend to take grass so much for granted! W. H. Hudson, that great lover of Nature, once wrote, " When I hear people say they have not found the world so interesting as to be in love with it, I am apt to think they have never really seen it—not even a blade of grass."

A friend who is an expert flower-arranger tells me her arrangements would not be half as effective if she simply used flowers; grasses always figure in her best displays.

Sunsets, mountain, rolling rivers—these are part of the majesty of Nature. But don't let's miss the beauty and wonder in a blade of grass.

THE FRIENDSHIP BOOK

JOHN FRANKLAND was one of the old school of country craftsmen. He was a village blacksmith in the Yorkshire district of Ryedale for over 70 years. No-one knew how many horses had been shod at his smithy, but when motor vehicles began taking over from horses, John turned to wrought-iron work.

One summer day two strangers to the village stood watching him working on an ornamental gate. One of them said, " We find it so nice to watch a real craftsman using his hands. We have a factory in the south of England and manufacture precision instruments."

" That's right," confirmed his companion. " Our sort of work is very, very precise. We have to work to an accuracy of one ten-thousandth of an inch."

" In that case," replied John, his eyes twinkling. " You'd better stay and watch. I'm exact."

ST CHRISTOPHER (whose festival day it is today) is thought of particularly as the patron saint of children because of the legend associated with him about carrying the Christ Child across a river ford.

But he is also the saint of wayfarers and, now, of motorists.

If you are travelling yourself today, or have friends or loved ones who are, you might like to remember, too, the old Gaelic blessing for travellers:

May a star lead you,
the wind be at your back,
the road rise to meet you,
and God hold you
in the hollow of His hand.

FRIDAY—JULY 26.

A QUAKER lady was once asked if she ever saw evil in anybody.

"Why, yes, dear, I see it," she said, "but I like to shut one eye and open the other only a little way if anything is wrong, because I like honey so much better than poison."

I think most of us would be glad to make the acquaintance of a woman who looks at life in that happy way.

SATURDAY—JULY 27.

F RED ASTAIRE, the great singing and dancing film star, was once asked the secret of his energy and young outlook when he was beyond 80. He replied simply, "I suppose it is because I approach everything as if it were fresh."

What a wonderful way of facing life! If we see only a sameness and dullness about life and about our surroundings, then of course we shall grow old and listless. It is not a bad idea to repeat to ourselves each morning when we wake:

New mercies each returning day
Hover around us while we pray.

. . . and having said it let us look for the newness which lies all about us. It is a matter of observation, of sensitivity, of having eyes and ears and minds alert to the wonder about us. Every day is a new day—there has never been one exactly like it before. Let us miss nothing of its wonder.

SUNDAY—JULY 28.

H E that is faithful in that which is least is faithful also in much.

THE FRIENDSHIP BOOK

A T the wedding of Prince Charles and Lady Diana Spencer in St Paul's Cathedral, the Archbishop of Canterbury, Dr Robert Runcie, reminded the bride and bridegroom (and us all) that, " Our faith sees the wedding day not as the place of arrival but as the place where the adventure really begins."

This idea of the importance of beginnings extends far beyond a wedding day, of course. We attach a good deal of importance—and rightly so—to ends, to results and achievements; yet if we thought only of those, there would be a good deal of disappointment and frustration. Beginnings can have an endless inspiration and stimulus for us. A new day, a new year, a new task, a new friendship, the opening of a new book, a new journey—if we really see these things as the beginnings of new adventures, life for us will be filled with wonder and surprise.

D R SAMUEL SMILES'S book " Self-help " is probably regarded by some as being very old-fashioned nowadays, but some of his sayings have a timelessness about them. For instance, " We learn wisdom from failure much more often than from success. We often discover what *will* do, by finding out what will not do; and probably he who never made a mistake never made a discovery."

T HOUGH yesterday was dreary
And today should bring its sorrow,
Make sure your heart is open
For the joy that comes tomorrow.

GOLDEN AGE

We all remember tranquil days
  When everything was right;
We store them in our memories
  And keep their image bright,
Sparing a moment now and then
To live those happy times again.

AUGUST

HOLD UP YOUR CHIN

PLUCK brings its reward,
Reverses don't kill,
If fate hits you hard
Strike back with a will.

Let it do what it can,
Still hold up your chin
For the world loves a man
Who never gives in.

A FEW doors from us is an elderly neighbour who had a serious illness a couple of years ago. It left him at first able to shuffle only as far as his garden gate with the aid of a walking frame, but there, in spite of his disability, he chatted cheerfully to anyone who would stop for a word with him—and most of them did. Then he became able to walk a little way along the road with two sticks, and then with the aid of only one.

I am sure part, at any rate, of the secret of his gradual recovery was his cheerful spirit. He talked about all sorts of things, but there was one mark of all these encounters. When you were about to leave him, he would touch your arm and say, " Just before you go, I have a funny story for you."

He always left me chuckling—and also remembering gratefully that " a merry heart doeth good like medicine ".

THE FRIENDSHIP BOOK

WHEN the Lady of the House and I were visiting friends in Staffordshire we came across this Mexican Prayer in the parish magazine of St Mary's, Rolleston-On-Dove:

I am only a spark, make me a fire,
I am only a string, make me a lyre,
I am only a drop, make me a fountain,
I am only an ant-hill, make me a mountain,
I am only a feather, make me a wing,
I am only a slave, make me a king.

SUFFER little children to come unto me, and forbid them not: for of such is the kingdom of God.

SORTING out some old books recently I came across a copy of " Alice's Adventures in Wonderland ". I couldn't resist browsing through the pages which gave me so much pleasure years ago.

You remember how the story starts with Alice sitting on a grassy bank beside her sister who was reading, but when she peeped at her sister's book it seemed very dull. " What is the good," thought Alice, " of a book without pictures or conversations?"

Pictures and conversations—what delight comes to us through our gifts of sight and hearing. As you give thanks for them you might also like to know a prayer I came across recently " for the blind, living in a world of colour, unable to see its splendours; for the deaf, living in a world of sound, unable to hear its harmonies; for the dumb, surrounded by voices, but unable to add their own."

TUESDAY—AUGUST 6.

DR HARRY EMERSON FOSDICK was the pastor of Riverside Church in New York City, and is remembered for many fine hymns and books. On one occasion his church caught fire and a great deal of damage was done. At once their Jewish friends at Temple Emmanuel offered their own premises for Christian worship.

Although the Riverside congregation offered to pay for the lighting, heating, and other bills, their Jewish hosts insisted that they would not take any money from their guests.

When the Riverside congregation eventually returned to their own church, the grateful worshippers sent the rabbi at Temple Emmanuel synagogue a large cheque. The rabbi promptly returned it.

" My dear fellow," Dr Fosdick telephoned the rabbi, " what a very Christian thing to do!"

The rabbi chuckled: " Oh no, what a very *Jewish* thing to do!"

WEDNESDAY—AUGUST 7.

YOU cannot pray the Lord's Prayer,
And even once say " I ";
You cannot pray the Lord's Prayer,
And even once pray " My ".
Nor can you say the Lord's Prayer
And not pray for another,
For when you ask for Daily Bread,
You can't miss out your Brother;
For others are included
In each and every plea.
From beginning to the end of it
It does not once say " Me ".

'MID THE FLOWERS

THE FRIENDSHIP BOOK

FOR over 50 years the entertainer, Percy Edwards, delighted audiences with his almost incredible imitations of birds and animals and brought his own love of nature to millions of people.

It is not surprising that when he appeared on a television programme in which he made a choice of favourite hymns, many of them were about the beauty and wonder of the natural world.

I was particularly impressed with his remarks about the hymn, " Morning has broken ".

" Wonderful!" he said, gazing up at the sky. " Wonderful variety. Never are two mornings alike. Newness. Freshness!"

Could there be a better thought with which to start each new day?

THERE is an old saying that " A mother's work is never done." Those of us who have gardens must feel that the same can be said of a gardener's work!

A friend of mine says he found that whenever he went to sit in his garden and enjoy a quiet half-hour, he was no sooner seated than he noticed some job that needed to be done—weeds to be pulled up, dead flower-heads to be removed, some fencing to be repaired and so on. He found that he was never sitting in his garden at all but simply working in it, so he decided that, one day a week, he would set apart a period to sit and enjoy it no matter what jobs presented themselves.

As W.H. Davies said,

What is this life if, full of care,
We have no time to stand and stare?

SATURDAY—AUGUST 10.

THE German philosopher, Ludwig Feuerbach, once said, " In the perishable petals of the flower there resides more spirit and life than in the great granite boulder which has defied the wear and tear of thousands of years."

True, there is a place in life for the great, strong, unchanging things. But I wonder if we sometimes tend to overlook the delight and inspiration which can come from frail and fleeting things—not only the flower which quickly fades, but the shy smile of a passing child, the sudden gleam of sunshine between the clouds, the silvery flash of a fish in a stream, Autumn leaves swirling past in the wind, falling snow flakes, the whiff of newly-baked bread as we pass the bakery, the sound of a passing band in the distance.

What sheer delight these frail and fleeting things can bring!

SUNDAY—AUGUST 11.

HE that hath, to him shall be given; and he that hath not, from him shall be taken even that which he hath.

MONDAY—AUGUST 12.

THE Lady of the House was visiting an elderly friend of ours and the conversation turned, as it so often does nowadays, to the rising price of things.

" I don't think all this decimal coinage business has helped," the old lady complained. " If the Lord had intended us to ' go decimal ' He would have given us only ten apostles instead of twelve."

I think the Lady of the House found difficulty in answering that!

TIMELESS

The world is at its finest
Where sea and sand unite
In harmony that's perfect,
Eternal, infinite.

L ORD ROBERTS was one of the ablest British soldiers of the 19th century. He was successful in campaigns against the tribesmen on the borders of Afghanistan, and in the Boer War recaptured many places which had been occupied by Boer forces, before handing over the command of the army to Lord Kitchener.

He was over 80 when the First World War broke out, but he wasn't content to stay out of the action. When Indian soldiers were detailed to fight in France, he felt impelled to go and greet them. However, on that visit he caught pneumonia and died.

For many, he will be remembered for the message printed inside the cover of the pocket Gospels which were distributed to the men of H. M. Forces. Dated 25th August 1914, it read: " I ask you to put your trust in God. He will watch over you and strengthen you. You will find in this little book guidance when you are in health, comfort when you are in sickness, and strength when you are in adversity."

It was signed simply " Roberts ".

WEDNESDAY—AUGUST 14.

A CHURCH newsletter which a friend sends me from time to time often contains what are titled " Ten Second Sermons." Here is a selection from a recent issue:

" The world looks brighter from behind a smile."

" Those who try to do something and fail are to be preferred to those who try to do nothing and succeed."

" Today is the tomorrow you worried about yesterday and all is well."

" The way to better your lot is to do a lot better."

THE FRIENDSHIP BOOK

A MUSING things happen everywhere—even in the police courts. For many years John Arthur Robert Cairns was a Metropolitan Police magistrate and on one occasion an elderly Irishman was brought before him, accused of being drunk and disorderly.

The defendant protested that he was not drunk, but hungry and weak from loss of sleep. He continued: " It was after enterin' a church I was, to ease the poor feet and sowl of me, but I thought I was not worthy to enter that holy place, and I lay down on the cowld stones before the door, and there it was I lay in an attitude of prayer, when the policeman hisself found me and locked me up."

" You say you were praying?" inquired Mr Cairns.

" Indade I was," came the reply. " Indade I was, yer Honour."

" You were holding a service by yourself, I take it?"

" That is so, yer Honour."

" Ah, well," murmured Mr Cairns, " we will now take up the collection. Seven and sixpence!"

W HEN I go on holiday I often reflect that if it had not been for the Christian church there might not have been any holidays at all. Centuries ago everybody worked throughout the year—except for Sundays and the Church festivals known as holy days. That's where our word ' holiday ' comes from, of course.

Though the original religious significance is often far from our minds, there is a special sense in which we ought to thank God for holidays. Don't you agree?

THE FRIENDSHIP BOOK

LOOK what I've found, Francis!" said the Lady of the House the other day, coming in triumphantly from the garden holding an avocado pear stone which was beginning to sprout. "This is the stone I pampered and cossetted and tried to grow indoors without result so I threw it out onto the rubbish heap—and look at it now! I must have given up too soon."

Too often we do, don't we?

WHOSOEVER exalted himself shall be abased; and he that humbleth himself shall be exalted.

MRS JOHNSON had just lost her husband. He had died after a long illness—and he was only in his late 50's. Should we call in and see her? Or would she think we were interfering? We hesitated, because we know that grief can be a very private thing, and visitors are not always welcome.

However, the Lady of the House and I decided we would call and see her—and we were so glad that we did. She was longing for someone to talk to, and spent an hour or so telling us of all the difficulties she had managed to overcome during her husband's illness, and all that their happy life together had meant . . . And then she apologised—for taking up so much of our time!

We left feeling that we had helped her, just by being there to listen. That, after all, is what friendship so often means, doesn't it? Just being willing to share each other's troubles.

WHAT'S THIS?

For children, everything is new
    And nothing has been done before;
There are so many things to do,
    So many wonders to explore.
Quite time enough in later days
To learn the grown-ups' curious ways.

IN 1907 when General Baden-Powell organised a little experimental camp for 20 boys on Brownsea Island in Poole Harbour, Dorset, he can have had little idea that he was starting the great international movement of Boy Scouts and Girl Guides—the most successful youth organisation the world has ever seen. When he later chose a motto for the Scouts it was one he borrowed from the police-force in South Africa where he had distinguished himself as a soldier—" Be Prepared!"

I always think this is a splendid motto—and not just for Scouts and Guides. Without becoming too anxious about the future, how right it is for all of us to make sensible practical preparations so that we can look ahead with confidence.

A NEIGHBOUR was telling me that one Sunday morning everything seemed to go wrong. First she overslept, then in the rush to get ready for church, she let the toast burn. To crown it all, when she pulled the door shut behind her she realised she had left her key inside. Deciding that she would have to leave that problem till she returned, she dashed to church just in time to seize her hymn-book from the attendant as the choir entered, and she gasped breathlessly, " It's just not my day today."

To her astonishment, the minister stood up at that moment and pronounced his call to worship, " This is the day which the Lord has made; we will rejoice and be glad in it."

Not *her* day, indeed, but God's day. What a difference it would make if we saw every day—particularly the difficult ones—in that light.

THE FRIENDSHIP BOOK

MARGARET BENTLEY, of Wyke, Bradford, wrote this poem which she dedicated "To Barbara."

> *Because you have been a friend*
> *In quiet ways,*
> *Because you brought gleams of hope*
> *On anxious days,*
> *Because you had time to listen*
> *When I poured out all my woe,*
> *Because you had troubles of your own*
> *And never let them show;*
> *Because you could still be cheerful*
> *In a world of haste and noise,*
> *Because you remembered little things,*
> *And shared your joys,*
> *Because, in the rough, tough game of life*
> *You kept your head held high,*
> *You made me rich in a thousand things*
> *That money will never buy.*

YOU may have heard the saying, " Barriers are for those who have no wings ". I like W. G. Branch's comment on this: " For those who *have* wings, most of the barriers cease to exist. A sparrow can triumph where an elephant would fail. As for the eagle, even mountain barriers melt away before its sunward flight."

Words worth remembering when we come up against some of the barriers most of us have to face at one time or another. If we have " wings "—courage, faith, hope, prayer, determination—then we can soar above the barriers of fear and difficulty, frustration and failure, which sometimes confront us.

I LIKE the story of the bus chugging along a country lane in Wiltshire. Suddenly it pulled up. The driver jumped out and ran up the path to a house. He knocked furiously at a window, and glared at the woman who came to it.

"Take that canary out of the window," he shouted to her, " this sun will kill it."

Having completed his good deed for the day, he returned to the bus, beamed happily at all his passengers, and continued the journey.

TAKE no thought for your life, what ye shall eat; neither for the body, what ye shall put on.

I HAVE just been reading the biography of the well-known Methodist preacher, the late Dr. W. E. Sangster, written by his son, Paul. I was amused by a story about the beginning of one of his early ministries in Colwyn Bay. He knew no Welsh, but thought it would be a nice idea to be able to give a greeting to his new congregation in Welsh. The words, " Borra da " (Good day) which he found in a Welsh phrase book seemed appropriate.

It so happened that on the Saturday before his first Sunday in his Welsh pulpit Mrs Sangster had bought some of that Welsh speciality, Bara brith, a fruit bread.

Unfortunately, Sangster became a little confused and as the congregation filed out of church the following morning each was surprised to be greeted with the words, " Bara brith "!

CONKER TIME

Every year with changing season
Children play their games anew,
As their parents did before them,
As their children, too, will do.

EVERYBODY knows the saying that " every cloud has a silver lining ", but I specially like the way in which Ellen Thorneycroft Fowler uses this familiar idea:

The inner half of every cloud
Is bright and shining;
I therefore turn my clouds about,
And always wear them inside out
To show the lining.

SUNDAY after Sunday the verger of a church found in the corner of a back pew a tiny screwed-up ball of paper. At first he threw them away, then one day he casually opened one. He found scribbled on it, " Laura—ill ". He looked at several more—" Rent. Mary's boy."; " Joe—no job. No letter from Mary."—and so on. Finally, he took them to the minister, telling him where he had found them. The minister knew they must have been written by a woman who always sat alone in the pew, and on the following Sunday he managed to speak to her as she was about to leave and gently asked if she would wait for a word with him. He showed her the notes and asked if there was any way he could help.

" You'll think it silly," she said, " but I saw an advertisement on a bus which said, ' Take your worries to church and leave them there.' I write the notes during the week, bring them to church and leave them there. I feel that God is taking care of them."

How right she was! We may not use scraps of paper, but many of us have found that when we walk out of a church, our worries are left behind.

THE FRIENDSHIP BOOK

EVERY nation seems to have a store of wisdom in its ancient proverbs. What profound truth there is in the old Indian saying, " Help thy brother's boat across and, lo!—thine own has reached the shore."

IT'S nice to feel someone is missing you, particularly when you're getting on a bit.

When Gran and Granpa Graham went from Newcastle to London to see their two-year-old grandson (and of course his father and mother!) little David thought they were wonderful. Every morning for several weeks he would dash into their bedroom as soon as he was awake and cosy down. It was just lovely for everybody.

Well, the happiest of visits must draw to a close. Gran and Granpa did their best to break the news to David that they were going, but he was too young to understand. The full meaning didn't dawn till the morning after they had left. His mother saw him dart into the bedroom and stare in disbelief when there was no Gran and Granpa. Just to make sure that they had really gone he got down on his knees and looked *under* the bed!

Gran and Granpa smiled when they heard the story, but secretly they were very moved. As I said, it's nice to know you're missed . . .

A SMALL boy was sitting with his father in church one Sunday and as the collection plate was passed round he was heard to whisper, " You don't have to pay for me, Daddy. I'm under five!"

SEPTEMBER

W HOSOEVER shall not receive the kingdom of God as a little child shall in no wise enter therein.

W HEN you're criticizing others,
And find faults here and there,
A flaw or two to speak of,
Or a weakness you can tear;
When you're blaming someone's meanness
Or accusing someone's self,
It's time that you went out to take
A walk around yourself.

There are many human failures
In the average of us all,
And many grave shortcomings
In the short ones and the tall;
But when we think of evils
Men should lay upon themselves,
It's time we all went out to take
A walk around ourselves.

We need so often in this life,
This balancing of scales,
This seeing how much in us wins
And how much in us fails;
But before you judge another,
Just lay him on the shelf,
The finest plan to follow is
To walk around oneself.

WOODLAND QUEEN

A graceful birch in summer leaf
Is clad in beauty rich and rare,
But, gilt by Autumn's Midas touch,
Its beauty is beyond compare.

THE FRIENDSHIP BOOK

ONE of the most famous rose-growers in the world was Harry Wheatcroft. He once said, " He who would grow good roses must have roses in his heart." So, it is not surprising to find that Harry Wheatcroft was not only a great grower of roses, but a great worker for world peace.

He wrote, " I deplore beyond all measure the thousands of millions spent to create implements to destroy mankind. With all that money everybody could grow roses. The world could be made so beautiful."

Idealistic? Sentimental? Perhaps; yet couldn't the world do with a bit of that idealism and sentiment? Roses in our gardens, in our homes, in our hearts. I like Harry Wheatcroft's vision.

TAXES! How we grumble about them! Someone has said that a government's chief aim is to impose taxes and the public's aim is to avoid them! When Michael Faraday first produced a continuous current through a moving conductor in a magnetic field (really, the first dynamo), Prime Minister Peel asked him what use it was. Faraday replied, " I don't know, but I wager that some day you will tax it!"

Taxes may be unpleasant, but they are a reminder of the part each of us must play in the life of the community, and the fact that we must pay for our privileges . . . and this extends far beyond taxation. It is when we accept this principle that we begin to understand what the Bible means when it says, " We are bound up together in the bundle of life."

We give and we receive—which of us would really have it any different?

THE FRIENDSHIP BOOK

MANY Negro pastors are noted for their simple, direct, down-to-earth approach in their preaching. They also often have a refreshing touch of humour which softens but does not make less effective the points they are trying to drive home to their listeners.

A good example of this is the sermon in which the preacher likened the members of his congregation to bones of various kinds. Some were " wish-bones " (always wishing, never doing); others were " jaw-bones " (the gossips), then there were the " dry bones " (prim and yet spiritually dead), and the " tail-bones " (always late!).

But those for whom he thanked God were the " back-bones " who threw themselves heart and soul into the life of the church and were always dependable.

ON a sunny day, if you passed by a certain Old Folks' Home in Scotland, you would see old Martha sitting smoking her clay pipe.

Martha was a tinker. She was pleased to pass the time of day with you, but you got the feeling that her thoughts were really far away, remembering the winding open road and the campfire and the voices of friends of long ago.

Well, Martha at last passed on. I don't suppose there were many people left who knew her, but someone remembered how she had spent her days before she came into the home and left a little posy of heather and wayside grasses to accompany her on her last journey.

Martha would have liked that, I am sure.

THE FRIENDSHIP BOOK

SATURDAY—SEPTEMBER 7.

WHEN bereavement hits us and there seems nothing left to live for, what do we do?

On the death of his much loved wife Jean, Joseph Cooper, whose TV series " Face The Music " gave so much pleasure, felt like withdrawing completely from programmes in which they had once been involved together.

He tells us in his life story what happened then. Jean's Aunt Barbara, who had always been deeply interested in his career, made one blunt statement which helped him more than all the words of comfort he had received:

" You either sink or swim and it is better for all concerned that you swim."

She spoke from experience, said Joseph Cooper, and she was a living example of her own philosophy.

SUNDAY—SEPTEMBER 8.

AS the clear light is upon the holy candlestick, so is the beauty of the face in ripe age.

MONDAY—SEPTEMBER 9.

I LIKE these words of advice sent to me by Mr P. J. Barsby of Attenborough, Nottingham:

Why is it that a friendly chat
Can often turn to spite,
Malicious gossip meant to show
A neighbour in bad light?

We should remember when we chat
That far from being smart,
Unfriendly gossip will degrade
A friendship from the start.

THE FRIENDSHIP BOOK

SOME time ago I heard a poem read on the radio. I haven't been able to trace the poem or its author, but snatches of it have remained with me ever since. It was about " music "—but not the kind of music that is written in a score or can be played upon an instrument. It was about sounds that give an uplift to the spirit. Among those the poet mentioned, which I remember, are happy laughter, a telephone call, and " thanks for what I did when I thought I had done nothing."

How endlessly we could add to these glad musical sounds if we would listen: the cries of children at play; the song of birds; the whisper of the wind in the trees; the bubbling of water as the kettle begins to boil; the ring of the doorbell when a friend calls; the rustle of leaves on the pavement on an autumn day; the plop of a letter when the postman calls; the clink of cutlery as the table is laid for a meal.

Yes, life is full of music, if we have ears to hear.

HENRY LONGHURST was a much-loved writer about golf. But he didn't just write about golf, for he saw the game as being like life in miniature.

" Golf isn't a fair game," he used to say. " But then, it was never meant to be a fair game."

The true test of a player, he explained, was what he did when a good shot ended where it was impossible to play the ball.

Life isn't fair, either. It's the ability to face misfortune—bereavement, unemployment, pain —that shows the sort of people we are. We can't steer clear of troubles but we can try, as Robert Burns said, " To have a heart above them all ".

THE FRIENDSHIP BOOK

THE Lady of the House has an elderly uncle who spends a few days with us from time to time. She loves to have him because she says that he is more appreciative of what is done for him, particularly for his meals, than any guest she knows.

He also has odd and original ways of expressing his gratitude. I think he excelled himself recently after a good breakfast, when he said, " Thank you, my dear. What a breakfast! It will take all day for my ribs to settle back into position!"

CAPTAIN Frederick Marryat's books are still enjoyed by many children. He knew that children like nothing better than a stirring tale. Yet it was only by chance that he started writing fiction.

As a 14-year-old boy he joined the Navy in Nelson's days. Before he had served six years, he had jumped overboard five times to save lives. When a boarding party was sent from the ship he often smuggled aboard so that he could take part in the action.

Those were the days of the press-gangs when young and able-bodied men were kidnapped and hustled aboard ships to take part in the wars. Marryat hated this practice so much that he wrote a book attacking it. As a punishment, he was sent to find a submerged rock in the middle of the Atlantic.

He did not find the rock, but he discovered his own talent for writing exciting tales. His success enabled him to start a new career as the author of such books as *Mr Midshipman Easy, Masterman Ready* and, in a different vein, *The Children of the New Forest*—books that can still thrill young and old.

A YOUNG boy came home from Sunday School and proudly showed to the family a Bible he had won for regular attendance. A friend of his mother's, who was by no means old, said, " Do you know, I remember I won a Bible for just the same thing when I was your age."

The youngster looked at her critically for a moment and then said, " I suppose that must have been the Old Testament "!

THE children of this world are in their generation wiser than the children of light.

KAREL KAPEK, the Czechoslovakian dramatist who wrote *The Insect Play,* popular in the 1930's, also wrote " A Gardener's Prayer ". Here are some extracts from it:

" Lord, grant that in some way it may rain every day, from about midnight until three o'clock in the morning, but it must be gentle and warm so that it can soak in.

" Grant that at the same time it would not rain on campion, alyssum, helianthemum, lavender and other drought-loving plants . . .

" And grant that the sun may shine the whole day long, but not everywhere (not, for instance, on spiraea or on gentian, plantain lily and rhododendron) and not too much."

That would be funnier, I think, if only most of us were not aware that too many of our prayers are like that, asking instead of offering.

REWARD

Trophies are fine—they do look nice
But what can compare with a lovely ice?

TUESDAY—SEPTEMBER 17.

I SUPPOSE if we look round about us as we walk about or go shopping we shall see people who look worried and harassed and sullen. A friend of ours has developed a very different technique—she looks for happy faces and kindly-looking people!

As she goes about she says to herself things like, " What a happy-looking woman there with those two children!" " What a cheerful old lady, in spite of hobbling with a stick!" " There's a pleasant-looking man!" " How those boys are enjoying themselves kicking that ball!"

She tells me it has given her a completely new outlook on life.

How about trying it for ourselves today?

WEDNESDAY—SEPTEMBER 18.

WHEN General William Booth, the founder of the Salvation Army, was an old man, his sight began to fail and after a short illness he became completely blind. His son, Bramwell, had the difficult task of telling him that he would never see again.

The old man was silent for several moments, and then he laid his hand upon his son's and said, " I have done what I could for God and for people with my eyes. Now I shall do what I can for God and for people without my eyes."

So often we think of what we could do if only we had this or that or the other opportunity. Yet much of the world's best work has been done by people in spite of—perhaps because of—their handicaps and limitations . . . Milton without his sight, Beethoven without his hearing, Bunyan without his liberty. Doesn't it make us feel ashamed sometimes at our own grumbling?

THE FRIENDSHIP BOOK

A FRIEND of ours is a nurse in an old people's ward of a hospital. She told us that the other day an old lady, new to the hospital and only just mobile, said to her, " I believe there is a television room, dear. Could you take me along there, please?"

" Yes, I will," said our friend, " but it is rather a long way down the corridors. I'll fetch a wheel-chair."

" No, no," said the patient. " I'll manage. Just you take my arm. I'll be all right." So, off they went, very slowly indeed, the old lady chatting away.

At last they reached the television room, and our nurse friend led the old lady to a comfortable chair with a good view of the television. " Oh, no," said the lady, " I don't want to stay. I don't really like television. I just wanted someone to talk to and you seemed such a nice, friendly person! You can take me back now, dear, and we will have another nice little chat on the way!"

All she wanted was someone to talk to. What a lot of people there must be like that—lonely folk for whom a few minutes of our time and talk will mean more than we can imagine.

A BUSINESS friend vouches for the truth of this story:

An office typist asked her friend who was similarly employed, " How do you like your new boss?"

" Oh, he's not bad," was the reply, " only he's kind of bigoted."

" How do you mean bigoted?" enquired the other.

" Well, he seems to think words can only be spelt *his* way."

THE FRIENDSHIP BOOK

WHETHER we realise it or not we all owe a debt to Luther Burbank, the American plant breeder who lived from 1849 to 1926 and developed many new varieties of fruit and flowers.

The motive behind his work was not wealth or fame. He once said, " I shall be content if, because of me, there can be better fruit, fairer flowers."

That's why I salute Luther Burbank.

BE ye therefore ready also: for the Son of man cometh at an hour when ye think not.

A FRIEND of ours who has been a semi-invalid for many years nonetheless preserves a cheerfulness of spirit which shames some of us who are much fitter than he is.

I once asked him what his secret was. He smiled and said, " Well, I don't know whether I can tell you that without breaking one of my rules! But perhaps, seeing it is you, Francis, I will."

He then went on to tell me that, years ago, he read a book which set down three simple rules to prevent ill-health getting one down.

" The first," he said, " is ' Refuse to talk about your health '. The more you talk about an ailment, even a common cold, the worse it seems to get! The second is, ' Refuse to worry about your health ' and the third is, ' Be genuinely grateful that your health is as good as it is '."

With a philosophy like that, is it any wonder he is one of the most cheerful men I have ever met?

I HEARD recently of two people who spent a day walking along part of the Ridgeway, that ancient track across the Berkshire Downs with its magnificent views and historical associations. Suddenly, across the grass an angry-looking man approached them. " Have you seen any mushrooms?" he demanded. They shook their heads in some surprise, and he stumped away crossly saying, " They told me I should find plenty and I haven't found one. It's been an absolute waste of time!"

A waste of time? On a beautiful day of sunshine and wind! Oh, yes, mushrooms have their place, and I happen to be very fond of them, but I think there were things up there on the Ridgeway that could have assuaged his disappointment if only he had let them. And it is usually so if we open our eyes and our minds.

WEDNESDAY—SEPTEMBER 25.

MARSHAL FERDINAND FOCH, French Commander-in-Chief of the Allied Forces in World War I, was once being entertained to dinner in Denver, Colorado. One of the speakers said that there was nothing but wind in French politeness, to which Foch retorted, " Nor is there anything but wind in a pneumatic tyre, yet it eases wonderfully the jolts along life's highway."

The simple courtesies of life *do* smooth the way for ourselves and others. Do you remember the words of Hilaire Belloc?

> *Of Courtesy, it is much less*
> *Than Courage of Heart or Holiness,*
> *Yet in my walks it seems to me*
> *That the Grace of God is in Courtesy.*

THE FRIENDSHIP BOOK

THERE was once a university professor who often said to his students, " As I was walking in my garden, pondering this lecture, the thought came to me that . . . "

Over and over he gave to them these thoughts which his garden inspired. One day two students went to tea with him and they asked to see his garden. To their amazement it was only a narrow strip of ground surrounded by high walls.

" Is this really the garden where you have all those inspiring thoughts, Doctor?" asked one of them.

" Why, yes," was the reply.

" But it's so small!" protested the student.

" Ah, yes," said the professor pointing to the sky, " but look how high it is!"

IT had been a wonderful season for apples. Wherever you went the trees seemed to be weighed down with fruit. In some gardens the ground was so thick with windfalls that the owners scarcely knew what to do with them.

One lady who lives in a house overlooking the beautiful park by the River Tweed, at Kelso in the Scottish Borders, solved the problem in the happiest way.

She put baskets laden with apples at her garden gate, with an invitation to passers-by: " Please help yourself."

Mrs Jane Morrison of Edinburgh, who was on holiday in Kelso, told me about this. She adds that, along with her holiday memories, she took home with her a lovely bag of apples — a delightful souvenir of the thoughtfulness of an unknown giver.

AT PLAY

A little water, a little sand,
Are every child's wonderland.

THE FRIENDSHIP BOOK

A CERTAIN Church of England dignitary went to preach at Boston parish church where, many years before, he had been curate. There he met a couple whose wedding he had conducted in 1948. They told him: " We always remember one thing you said in your address that day."

The clergyman was delighted, and wondered which words of wisdom had survived the years. They replied: " You said we probably wouldn't remember a word you'd said . . ."

A MAN'S life consisteth not in the abundance of the things he possesseth.

IN her book " Medieval People ", the historian Eileen Power has what sounds at first reading a very strange sentence. She writes, " Marco Polo discovered China when he was alive, and after he was dead, discovered America." What she means is that when Christopher Columbus read " Marco Polo's Travels " his imagination was so fired that it set him off on his journey westward which led *him* to the discovery of America. But in a sense, Marco Polo was responsible, too!

One doesn't need to be an explorer to know this kind of experience. Inspiration is a two way traffic. How much we ourselves owe to things we have read, or heard, or seen in connection with other people. It works the other way, too. We never know what inspiration our own words and deeds may provide for others.

OCTOBER

TUESDAY—OCTOBER 1.

WE sometimes say, " It isn't what you say that matters, so much as how you say it." How true that is! In one of his books, Dr James Bender, a noted speech authority, asks, " Is your ' Good morning ' really good? Are your ' Congratulations!' enthusiastic? Does your ' How are you?' sound interested?"

What a power for good we all possess by the *lively* use of words like these. " Your words have kept men on their feet," says a character in the book of Job in the Bible. With a simple, warm, heart-felt greeting you and I can gladden many a soul today!

WEDNESDAY—OCTOBER 2.

OH, I'm just a housewife." How often one hears this. New brides are perhaps the worst offenders. They seem almost duty-bound to let you know that they are now *only* housewives.

What a very good thing for us that young Marie Curie did not turn away from her vitally important work with radium, and say, " Oh, I won't bother now that I'm a housewife."

Her home was shabby, and the small boxroom where she worked long hours with her husband Pierre was nothing like a modern laboratory, but Marie's steadfast courage and sheer determination led to one of the most important breakthroughs in medical science.

Countless lives have been saved, and great suffering has been eased because of the magnificent work done by Madame Curie—housewife!

THE FRIENDSHIP BOOK

FRIENDSHIP is the theme of these verses sent to me by Mrs G. B. Taylor of Foster, Quebec, Canada:

> *I know what every woman needs*
> *As she perchance grows older:*
> *A true and understanding friend*
> *To lend a wetproof shoulder.*
> *And who, when they shall meet again*
> *Forgets the things she told her!*

———

> *A rare, precious thing*
> *Is a close friend tie,*
> *A wellspring of happiness*
> *Ever near by.*

I WONDER how present-day workers would feel if, at the end of the week they were handed a bag of salt for their labours. Not very pleased, I imagine!

Yet the soldiers of the Roman legions were paid partly in salt and the very word " salary " comes from " salarium," meaning " soldier's salt money."

Wars have been fought over salt. One of the reasons the Romans came to Britain was that they had been told the country was rich in it. Some of the first known roads were built to transport salt, and bars of salt were once used as currency in Ethiopia.

Yes, salt is one of the commonest yet most important minerals in the world.

Why do I mention this? Just because it strikes me from time to time that I—and perhaps some other people—take too many everyday blessings for granted.

THE FRIENDSHIP BOOK

A DAILY newspaper published some interesting statistics about a Summer season at an East Coast holiday resort. It appears that 88 people were stung by jellyfish, eight bitten by dogs, 100 stung by insects, 26 trapped their fingers in deck chairs and—somewhat surprisingly—nine were bitten by monkeys.

"But," added the paragraph, "there was some good news. For the first time for years, no-one was bitten by a donkey."

There is always something to be grateful for!

IF a kingdom be divided against itself, that kingdom cannot stand.

NOT far from Morecambe, on the Lancashire coast, there is the historic hamlet of Sunderland Point, which was once an important cotton post. I recently made a pilgrimage to a lonely grave there—that of the Negro slave who died in 1796, having come to England on one of the cotton ships. This is the touching epitaph carved on his grave-stone:

Here lies poor Sambo
A faithful Negro attending his master
  from the West Indies.
Died on his arrival at Sunderland.
But still he sleeps till the awakening Sounds
Of the Archangel's Trumpet new Life impart
Then the great Judge his Approbation founds
Not on a Man's Colour, but his warmth of Heart.

THE FRIENDSHIP BOOK

MOST of us know of Charles Kingsley as the author of stories such as " The Water Babies " and " Westward Ho!", but he had many other claims to fame, for he was the faithful vicar of the parish of Eversley in Hampshire where he visited his people daily, the Professor of Modern History at Cambridge, a social reformer greatly interested in the conditions of the poor and of the gipsy community, and a prolific writer on social subjects.

This ever-active man was clearly writing out of his own experience when he said, " Thank God every morning when you get up that you have something to do that day which must be done whether you like it or not. Being forced to work and forced to do your best will breed in you . . . diligence and strength of will, cheerfulness and content and a hundred virtues which the idle never know."

IT'S a wonderful thing to be brought up in a home where there is always music to be heard—even if, when we are very young, we don't quite understand what some of the musical terms mean.

I am thinking of a story of that much-loved lady of oratorio, Dame Isobel Baillie. When she was five years old she heard of a family friend who had been given an encore at a local concert. Early next morning she was round at the singer's door. " Please may I see your encore," she said.

That little girl, in days to come, was to have many happy experiences of the meaning of the word encore. Her stage appearances thrilled audiences the world over, while her famous recording of " I Know That My Redeemer Liveth " has brought joy to thousands.

I LOVE the quaint sayings of children in which they say things not quite as adults would and yet making clear to us just what they mean.

A young son of a neighbour of ours had not had a bicycle very long, and returning from a short trip he was greeted rather anxiously by his mother. " I hope you were very careful, Billy."

" Oh, yes, I was, Mum," was the reply. " I slowed at the ' Slow ' sign, halted at the ' Halt ' sign and bended at the ' Bend ' sign!"

M ISS M. WATTS of Cove, Farnborough, sent me a charming poem titled " My Friends " from which I quote these verses:

Over the years I've made many friends,
Friends I hold most dear.
Some I shall never see again,
As I shed a silent tear.

Like me, my friends have older grown
And as the years go by,
Friendship links another year
And stronger grows the tie.

Now friendship is the greatest gift
And, when you are growing old,
Friends like the ones that I have got,
Are worth their weight in gold.

A handshake here, a handshake there,
A kiss upon the cheek;
A smile that says I love you still,
No need for one to speak.

JUST THINK . . .

Can you imagine how dull it would be
To dwell in a country without any sea?
How lucky we are to have shores that extend
From far John o' Groats to remotest Land's End,
With beaches and cliffs and all manner of ports
And fine, sandy bays for our holiday sports.

THE FRIENDSHIP BOOK

CLEVER men can sometimes be too clever. We are told that the philosophers of the Middle Ages argued seriously about the number of angels who could stand on the point of a pin!

But all great truths are simple. You may agree with me that Confucius summed it all up 2500 years ago.

He was asked: " What is knowledge?"

He answered: " Knowing people."

He was asked: " What is humanity?"

He answered: " Loving people."

SUNDAY—OCTOBER 13.

THE wolf also shall dwell with the lamb, and the leopard shall lie down with the kid.

MONDAY—OCTOBER 14.

THAT great star of the theatre, Ivor Novello, was one of the most generous of men. His phenomenal output of songs such as " We'll Gather Lilacs " and shows like " King's Rhapsody " earned him large sums, much of which he used to help people in need. Some of them he supported on a permanent basis and when his secretary became alarmed by the monetary outgoings, Ivor told her that whatever else should be cut, these cheques must never be reduced as they were depended upon.

His helping hand is still at work for he left most of his fortune and the royalties from performances of his music to theatrical charities and he gave his country house as a rest home for old actors and actresses. Truly he will be remembered as a great composer and the kindest of men.

A FEATURE of many stately homes open to the public is the portrait gallery showing the members of the family which owned the house through the years.

But at Erddig House at Clwyd in Wales the Lady of the House and I came across an interesting and unusual exception. The Yorke family, who lived at Erddig for nearly two and a half centuries, had more portraits and photographs of their employees than of the family. Indeed, they even wrote verses in appreciation of them, of which there is a huge collection!

For instance:

Two sisters of the name of Trevor
United here in one endeavour,
Each working for the general good
In laundry and preparing food.

A lovely tribute.

MY friend Peter's young son is quite brilliant at school but he is not the most observant of young men.

" Why are you wearing odd socks?" his mother asked him the other evening.

He looked down. " Oh, dear," he said. " I think one of the pair must have got lost in the wash."

" If you look in your bedroom drawers," his mother suggested, " I'm sure you'll find the odd sock."

" I'll have a look," he said.

" He was back in a few minutes. " I didn't find an odd sock," he told her. " But I did find another pair just like the ones I'm wearing!"

THE FRIENDSHIP BOOK

PHYLLIS BIRCHALL of Warfield, near Bracknell, sent me several lovely poems of which this is one.

TAKE HEART

Do not despair when things look grey, just hold your courage high, it may be bad but stick it out you'll win through by and by. For life is full of ups and down, not roses all the way, and even though a cloud appears, keep smiling come what may. Don't think that you're the only one who's had it really rough, there's lots of people in the world who've had more than enough. But strength is given by unseen hands if you will stop and pray, and God will lead you through the storm towards a brighter day.

THE only way of knowing where a shoe pinches is to wear it.

That is why Frank Jennings left his comfortable home and roughed it as a tramp. For three to four months annually, for many years, he tramped the highways of England, sleeping under hedges and in flea-ridden beds in lodging-houses. The help he gave to down-and-outs he met on the road earned him the title, " The Tramps' Parson ".

In his autobiography, he wrote:

" Throughout the years, I have sought to offer friendship on the road to my fellow-travellers. Early in life I came to see that it was only the kind heart, the encouraging word and the generous deed that put sanity and purpose into life. Human existence can be very desolate, bereft of a passing handshake, a concerned inquiry, a chummy smile. Pity and need make all flesh kin."

THE FRIENDSHIP BOOK

VIVIAN BIRD, a well-known Midlands author and journalist, is a great walker, now in his sixties. When he was 47 he underwent a serious cancer operation and many thought this would be the end of his walking days. But not so. Indeed, he claims that he walked himself back to health, and to celebrate his 50th birthday he walked 50 miles in one day! In praise of the health-giving power of walking he quotes the historian, G. M. Trevelyan, " I have two doctors—my left leg and my right!"

Yet was it *just* walking which restored Vivian Bird? Surely behind the walking was an indomitable spirit and faith. If we can't emulate the walking we can have a shot at the faith.

THE parched ground shall become a pool, and the thirsty land springs of water.

HAVE you ever fumed and fretted when someone was late for an appointment? You probably got more and more angry and were soon thinking you were being very badly treated.

Albert Einstein, perhaps the greatest scientist of this century, didn't let such things bother him. This good-natured genius was prepared to talk to anyone.

" Why should I mind that you are late meeting me?" he once said. " Am I less capable of reflecting on my problems here than at home? Here " (he took out a much-chewed pencil) " is my laboratory."

So often it is true that the greatest men and women are the most humble.

THE FRIENDSHIP BOOK

HE'S dead. Pablo Casals is dead." The news spread round the world on October 22nd, 1973. This famous Spanish-born cellist, composer and conductor had seemed as if he would achieve his century, but he missed it by three years.

In 1950 he told a reporter the " secret " of his vivid life. " Every day I am reborn and every day I must begin again."

This philosophy kept him young. So did his interest in young people and children. He once stated: " Each little child must be told ' Do you know what you are? You are a marvel. You are unique. In all of the world there is no other child exactly like you—you may become a Shakespeare, a Michelangelo, a Beethoven. You have the capacity for anything.' "

Casals believed that if only each child were to realise this, then wars and bitterness would cease.

Only a short time before his death he told a New York audience: " I am an old man, but in many senses a young man. And this is what I want you to be, young, young, all your life . . . "

SOME friends of ours had been enduring rotten weather—heavy rain, hail, sleet, the lot. Then, one night, there was a terrible thunderstorm—the lightning seemed to flash all night, and the rumble of the thunder kept Betty awake, unlike her husband who slept through it all.

Next morning she told him all about it.

" Well, I never," commented Joe. " Why on earth didn't you wake me? You know I can't sleep when it thunders."

THE FRIENDSHIP BOOK

HOW many of the irritating and frustrating experiences of life would be diminished if we could learn to laugh at them! Annoying as it is to have a long wait for a bus, I have never got as hot under the collar about it since I read the humorist A. A. Thomson on the subject.

He said that if he went to catch a bus, all buses on the route where he waited ceased to run, while in the opposite direction buses ran merrily by in convoys of six or eight! " I can," he wrote, " disintegrate the whole bus service of central London merely by standing at a request bus stop."

He further maintained that if he went into a restaurant he immediately became invisible to waitresses!

See the funny side of things and life loses a lot of its petty irritation.

ONE of the greatest—some think *the* greatest—of English landscape painters, was John Constable, famous for such paintings as " Flatford Mill ", " The Hay Wain ", " Salisbury Cathedral " and many others.

Yet in his own day Constable had a hard struggle for recognition and when he died most of his pictures were in his own possession, unsold.

Still, neither neglect nor praise greatly affected Constable. Something of his strong character is revealed in these words he once wrote: " The landscape painter must walk in the fields with a humble mind. No arrogant man was ever permitted to see nature in all her beauty."

And that goes for all of us—painters or not.

<u>SATURDAY—OCTOBER 26.</u>

A SUNDAY School teacher told me rather ruefully that she had spent a lot of time telling a class of children the meaning of the parable of the Good Samaritan, then, when she asked one child to explain it she received the reply, " It means that when I am in trouble people ought to help me!"

Unfortunately there are people who think like that—just as there were at the time of the Samaritan himself. Things don't really change all that much, do they?

<u>SUNDAY—OCTOBER 27.</u>

THEN the eyes of the blind shall be opened, and the ears of the deaf shall be unstopped.

<u>MONDAY—OCTOBER 28.</u>

THE church magazine was called " Outlook ", surely a splendid title, indicating the nature of the work of the church. But, on the front cover was a picture of the inside of the church—empty pews and all!

This inward look when we ought to be looking outwards and reaching out in helpfulness, is a weakness not only of some churches but also of many of us as individuals. We are so often wrapped in our own concerns and lost in self-pity, when we could find release by helping others.

Lady Masham was seriously injured in a riding accident many years ago and, as a result, was confined to a wheelchair. Instead of repining, she threw herself into helping other disabled people, thus not only helping many, but finding for herself the joy of service.

I FORGET now just how it arose, but in a conversation with our old friend Mary I happened to remark, " You know what they say, Mary—tomorrow never comes."

" Well, that's all right by me," said Mary. " I've had today!"

I think I have said before that I consider Mary to be a bit of a philosopher!

HERE is a chuckle from an older reader for all others who are getting on a bit:

My hearing aid is excellent,
My dentures never pain;
Bifocals fit me splendidly,
But I sometimes miss my brain!

IN one of his many books about the English countryside, its people and customs, that much-travelled writer, J. H. B. Peel, has a passage about festivals — May Day, Hallowe'en and the like. Some people, he says, will dismiss them as valueless superstition, but he takes a different view.

" Many customs," he says, " are echoes from an England that was merrie, not in a tipsy but in the sober meaning of that word, which implies a willingness to take both the rough and the smooth without being bowled over by either of them. The best of these customs add tuppenceworth of colour to the penny-plainness of life."

How grateful we should be for anything which does just that.

NOVEMBER

FRIDAY—NOVEMBER 1.

THERE is an old saying, "Cornwall has more saints than heaven itself!" You cannot go far in that county, as the Lady of the House and I have found, without coming across a church, a well or a village bearing the name of a saint you have probably never heard of—St Piran, St Rumon, St Ia, St Petroc, St Uni and a host of others.

When we think of saints we usually do so in terms of haloes and stained-glass windows, and people of extraordinary piety. But in the Bible, Paul uses the word to describe the members of the church—ordinary people who have been called to serve and worship God.

Today, All Saints Day, is a good time to remind ourselves that though we may be far from perfect, we *all* have our part to play in making the world a better place.

SATURDAY—NOVEMBER 2.

I READ recently of a group of schoolboys who claimed to be the country's "worst football team"! They had hundreds of goals scored against them and had never won a match. But they still went on playing because they loved the game.

I think they have a lot to teach us—about life, if not about football! They remind me of an anonymous prayer I once jotted down:

> *Not the quarry, but the chase,*
> *Not the laurel but the race,*
> *Not the hazard, but the play,*
> *Make me, Lord, enjoy alway.*

THE FRIENDSHIP BOOK

THE grass withereth, the flower fadeth, but the word of our God shall stand for ever.

THE other day, when the Lady of the House and I were visiting our old friend Mary, she said, " How do you like my flowers?" and then, before we could comment on the vase of blooms on the table, she added, " These are the most expensive flowers in the world!"

I must confess they looked pretty ordinary to me and I looked questioningly at Mary. Then she went on to explain that a friend had brought them from her tiny garden. Flowers were almost over and she had quite a job to gather together a respectable bunch.

" It's the very last bunch in the garden," she told Mary, " and I wanted you to have them."

" That's why I call them ' expensive '," said Mary. " I reckon I'm right, don't you?"

I certainly do!

THE Lady of the House and I have a friend—by no means young—who is a real outdoor man. Nothing can keep him from his daily walk. Rain, hail or snow, you will find him, suitably clad, marching up the road.

Once, when I commended him on his hardiness, he replied with a smile, " Ah, well, Francis, there is no such thing as bad weather. It's just that sometimes it's better than others!"

I think you can face most things—not only the weather—with a philosophy like that!

MARION ELLIOTT of York sent me a copy of her book of poems, *The Two Gardens*. From the many lovely things in it I have chosen this one, called " God's Plans."

> *We are not always ready*
> *For the things that God has planned;*
> *They are sometimes unexpected*
> *And we do not understand.*

> *But always there's a purpose*
> *Which as yet we may not see;*
> *It's locked away from vision,*
> *But God's love provides the key.*

MOST people have heard of the model villages such as New Lanark, Bournville and Port Sunlight built for their workers. Another was Saltaire in Yorkshire built in the middle of the 19th century by Sir Titus Salt, the worsted manufacturer.

In addition to 22 streets named after his children and grandchildren there was a school, a library, an institute, a hospital and, perhaps most impressive of all, a Congregational (now United Reformed) Church. It is a replica of a church which Salt saw on his Italian travels, symbolising the religion at the heart of his life, as of his village.

A feature of the building is a tiny gallery at the back. It was originally intended as a family pew for the Salts, but Titus rarely used it. He preferred to sit among the members of the congregation rather than in splendid isolation. A great man, but a humble one, and when he died he was still " among the people," for 40,000 gathered to line the streets for his funeral.

NICE AND SHARP

*Many ancient skills are gone
    In these machine-made days,
But there are craftsmen with us yet
    Using the good old ways.*

THE FRIENDSHIP BOOK

THE most famous description of Hell is surely that given by the great Italian poet, Dante, in his " Inferno ". Do you know that Dante considered that the very worst people are not those who do wicked things, but those who fail to speak out against wickedness?

" The hottest places in Hell," he wrote, " are reserved for those who in times of great moral crises maintain their neutrality."

It's important to be charitable and tactful, but there *are* times when we need to speak out for what we know to be right.

MANY years ago the villagers of Grosslawitz in Germany built a new church with the labour of their own people and money from their own pockets. However, there was not enough money to purchase a bell and the people didn't know what to do.

Then the local schoolmaster saw something which gave him an idea—it was two or three stalks of wheat growing in a hedge. He asked the chidren in the village school not to touch them, but to share his plan with their parents. This was to plant the grain from those stalks in his garden, and the following year to reap and plant again. They did this and in two years his garden would not hold all the grain, so several local farmers offered corners of fields where the schoolmaster's wheat could flourish.

Then came the harvest when there was enough to sell. The proceeds were sufficient to buy the longed for bell.

Remember what the Bible says, " Who has despised the day of small things?"

SUNDAY—NOVEMBER 10.

THE Lord gave, and the Lord hath taken away; blessed be the name of the Lord.

MONDAY—NOVEMBER 11.

OUTSIDE was silver. Inside was gold." This is the intriguing opening sentence of Eric Malpass's novel, " Sweet Will ", based on the life of William Shakespeare.

The silver is the street outside, bathed in moonlight; the gold is the glow of candlelight in the cosy dwelling-room of an Elizabethan cottage.

Silver and gold! The varied life of the world about us, the comfort and security of our own homes. How wealthy we are!

TUESDAY—NOVEMBER 12.

PLACED in the outside wall of Skipton's ancient parish church is a tombstone to members of the Longfellow family, one of whom was uncle to the famous American poet.

Inside the church are many fine monuments and memorials, but one of the most telling and simple is a little framed prayer:

Holy God who madest me
And all things else to worship thee,
Keep me fit in mind and heart
Body and soul to take my part,
Fit to stand and fit to run,
Fit for sorrow, fit for fun,
Fit for work and fit for play,
Fit to face life day by day.
Holy God who madest me,
Make me fit to worship Thee.

THE FRIENDSHIP BOOK

WE have all felt anxiety sometimes for loved ones far away, but what must it be like for an astronaut's wife as her husband whirls round in space?

Here is what Mrs Alan Shepard, wife of America's first astronaut said, as her husband was launched on that great adventure into the unknown: " I believe in the power of good and of God. I felt goodness all around me and I knew that Alan was in his right place and that he was in the hands of God. I slept well . . . "

Someone else has said, very similarly, " Think good and think God, then all will be well—very well indeed!"

SOME rather rude things have been said at times about committees! For instance, " A committee is an organisation which keeps minutes and wastes hours " or, " The ideal committee is a committee of two of which one member is permanently ill!" Then there is the definition, " A committee is a group of people who, individually able to do nothing, get together to decide collectively that nothing can be done!"

But of course, despite their weaknesses, committees have the great value of enabling people to talk things over together and to see each other's point of view.

This is often a great help, and we don't need to be on a committee to secure such benefits. A group of friends can serve this purpose; so can the family circle. Our troubles are often halved when we talk them over with someone else.

MY friend Lorna once bought a canary but was concerned when the assistant put it in a small cardboard box. The box had a few holes at each end but the bird was in almost complete darkness.

" I couldn't get home fast enough," Lorna told me later. " I was so worried about the little bird crouching in the dark. I scrambled on to a bus and held the box on my lap. Then to my surprise the canary started to sing. Its lovely music filled the bus and the other passengers were sorry when I got off."

I like that story of a brave little bird. It had no idea what was happening, where it was going or what fate awaited it, but it faced uncertainty with a song.

None of us knows what tomorrow will bring, whether the skies will be dark or bright, but it does help if we, too, can face the unknown with a smile and a song.

A CHURCH member complained to his minister, after yet another financial appeal had been made, " The trouble with this church is that it's Give! Give! Give! all the time."

The minister looked for a moment at the complainer and then said quietly, " Thank you. That's the best definition of Christianity I have heard."

Yes, and not just of Christianity but of life itself; nor, of course, is it just a matter of money. Life's richness is not in getting and having, but in giving and sharing—happiness, friendship, good counsel, experience.

What a lot we all have to give!

THE FRIENDSHIP BOOK

THE wilderness and the solitary place shall be glad for them; and the desert shall rejoice and blossom as the rose.

I DON'T know who it was—but how I should like to have met the man of whom it was said, " Give him a laundry list and he will set it to music!"

The world is made a happier place for us all by people who go cheerfully about the sometimes rather dull and drab activities of life and, so to speak, bring music out of them. May we be numbered among them.

THERE is an old Jewish legend of a peasant and his family who had to sleep in the same room as the hens. He went to ask the local rabbi for advice about his problem and to his astonishment was told to add a goat and a cow to the already overcrowded room.

Perplexed, but obedient, he returned home. After a fortnight he could stand it no longer and went back to the rabbi complaining that things were now intolerable.

" All is well, my son," smiled the Rabbi. " Your troubles are at an end. Go home and take away the cow!"

If it seems an unlikely story it is certainly a great lesson in contentment. The peasant, grumbling about a few hens, had never stopped to think how much worse things could be. It's a lesson I'm sure we could all ponder.

THE FRIENDSHIP BOOK

IT takes two to make a friendship but perhaps only one to start it. This little rhyme, sent to me by a reader in Banffshire, will show what I mean.

> *If after church you wait awhile,*
> *Someone will greet you with a smile.*
> *Though if you quickly rise and flee*
> *We'll all seem stiff and cold maybe.*
> *The one beside you in the pew*
> *Is, perhaps, a stranger, too.*
> *All here, like you, have fears and cares.*
> *All of us need each other's prayers.*
> *In fellowship we bid you meet*
> *With us around God's mercy seat.*

LIKE most people, the Lady of the House and I each have our favourite chair. They are not Chippendales, Hepplewhites or anything like that—just plain, homely but very comfortable chairs. The Lady of the House sometimes says of hers, " It's like a home within a home!"

The country writer H. J. Massingham once had a yew armchair lovingly and painstakingly made for him by a local craftsman. He said he could never sit in it without thinking of the beauty of the forest from which it came and the loving care with which it was made. " Somehow," he said, " you couldn't think of anyone sitting in that chair and uttering trivial or unkind or angry words—only words and thoughts of love and gentleness and truth seemed to fit that chair."

A bit fanciful? Perhaps. But then our favourite chair is a kind of refuge, a place of peace and gentleness and gratitude.

L ITTLE Billy, our neighbour's small boy, has been up to his jokes again. He had been shopping for his mother and as he passed our gate he called out to me as I was working in the garden. Waving a parcel he said, " I'm on a sea-food diet, Mr Gay."

I thought this was rather an odd thing for a small boy to say, but before I had time to answer he followed it up with, " I see food and eat it."

One up again for young Billy!

E VERY three years a number of ambitious young pianists gather for the Leeds International Pianoforte Competition.

Its founder and chairman, Miss Fanny Waterman, herself an internationally famous piano teacher, has spoken about the requirements of the competitors—sheer stamina and technical skill, but also what she calls " visionary ideas about music." She explains, " You have to be a musical detective because the composer has only written little black notes and a few instructions and you have to conjure up in sound what you think Beethoven, for example, meant at the time he lived."

It is those " visionary ideas " which can lift a pianist from the good to the great. But a bit of vision, a bit of imagination, could transform life for most of us. The writer of the book of Proverbs in the Bible said, " Where there is no vision the people perish."

T HE sabbath was made for man, and not man for the sabbath.

THE FRIENDSHIP BOOK

I WAS walking home the other night with a young man who was telling me that at his youth club he had just met a new member and he was sure they were going to be great friends.

" It was strange," he said. " There we were—we had never met. And yet in five minutes we were friends."

Then he added, " I suppose most friends were once strangers. It makes you think, doesn't it ?"

It certainly set me thinking of the many different ways in which the most important friendships in my life were formed. And perhaps this young man's remark will set both you and me thinking of the chances that come our way almost every day to add new friendships to old.

JOHN HILLABY'S book " Journey Through Britain " tells how he walked from Land's End to John o' Groats.

Somewhere on the England-Wales border he met an old man who asked him where he had come from. Hillaby told him how far he had come and the old man said, " Do you mean to tell me you have *walked* all the way here ?"

Hillaby told him he had and the man shook his head sadly and said, " Then all I can say is it's a pity you couldn't be doing something more useful."

But what *is* useful? Exercise, fresh air, contemplation of the beauties of Nature, meeting with fresh people, seeing fresh places, learning about his own country and its history—these were but a few of the things Hillaby had gained. Were all these not " useful "?

I'M HERE!

My mistress loves to read a book
And often lets me sit and look,
But I make sure she won't forget
A girl's best friend's a faithful pet.

THE FRIENDSHIP BOOK

ONE of the most popular songs of a few generations ago was, "Home, sweet home". Most of us, I imagine, have heard it and sung it some time or other. But I wonder how many know of its origin.

The man who wrote it, John Howard Payne, was a poor, homeless wanderer. On one occasion, without sufficient in his pocket to buy himself a meal or a bed for the night, he passed a brightly-lit house in London. Through the windows he glimpsed a scene of warmth and happiness which inspired him to write his famous song. Whether it brought him fortune I do not know. It has certainly brought inspiration and gratitude to countless people.

THE early days of married life can present problems even to the most perfectly matched man and woman. But when bride and bridegroom push themselves up the aisle of the church in wheelchairs, knowing that that is how they will pass the rest of their days, then the difficulties of married life seem almost too great.

But to Richard and Sandra Creed, chairbound since infancy, love for each other and faith in God was sufficient. In a most moving little book, "Together for God", they looked back on the first ten years of their married life, years full of sunny days though not without grey ones, too.

One bit of advice they offer to all married couples: "Don't behave in such a way today as to live in a world of regret tomorrow."

Simple, isn't it? But those few words say everything about the understanding that must exist for a marriage to be a happy one.

THE FRIENDSHIP BOOK

SOON after his enthronement as Archbishop of Canterbury, Dr Robert Runcie used this lovely old prayer which Henry Wadsworth Longfellow adapted from the Spanish of the 16th-century Saint Teresa:

> *Let nothing disturb thee,*
> *Nothing affright thee,*
> *All things are passing*
> *God never changeth.*
> *Patient endurance*
> *Attaineth to all things;*
> *Whom God possesseth*
> *In nothing is wanting*
> *—Alone God sufficeth.*

JOHN WARD grew up in the Moston area of Manchester and later wrote the story of his hometown.

One day, as a little boy, he was wandering along the country lanes and stopped to examine a wayside plant. He didn't know what it was, but in a few moments old Sal Dawson came on the scene. She was a tall, gaunt woman with sharp, inquisitive eyes. She was a local " character " with a lot of strange ways, and many folk were, in fact, a little afraid of her. But John Ward, recollecting in later years the way she came up to him, remarked: " There must have been grace in her soul, or she could not have talked to a little boy and told him the name of a plant growing on the highway side. I never forgot the name of the little blue selfheal after that meeting."

By such small acts of simple kindness are folk remembered.

DECEMBER

SUNDAY—DECEMBER 1.

THEY shall beat their swords into plowshares, and their spears into pruninghooks; nation shall not lift up sword against nation, neither shall they learn war any more.

MONDAY—DECEMBER 2.

TODAY let us say together some of the lovely words of " A Nun's Prayer ":

Lord, Thou knowest better than I know myself that I am growing older and will some day be old. Keep me from the fatal habit of thinking I must say something on every subject and on every occasion. Release me from craving to straighten out everybody's affairs. Make me thoughtful but not moody: helpful but not bossy. With my vast store of wisdom, it seems a pity not to use it all, but Thou knowest, Lord, that I want a few friends at the end . . .

I dare not ask for grace enough to enjoy the tales of others' pains but help me to endure them with patience. I dare not ask for improved memory, but for a growing humility . . . Teach me the glorious lesson that occasionally I may be mistaken.

Keep me reasonably sweet, I do not want to be a saint—some of them are so hard to live with—but a sour old person is one of the crowning works of the devil.

Give me the ability to see good things in unexpected places, and talents in unexpected people. And give me, O Lord, the grace to tell them so.

AMEN.

TUESDAY—DECEMBER 3.

HELPING in the church Jumble Sale, the Lady of the House was surprised to see a friend pounce upon an old-fashioned iron of the kind that had to be heated on the fire on washing day.

" I expect you wonder what on earth I want this for," she smiled, " but I have started a little collection of domestic ' bygones ' on a shelf in my kitchen. They're nice to look at, of course, but they have another purpose. When my household chores begin to get me down, I glance at these old things and think what a lot of drudgery we are saved nowadays. They make me feel very grateful."

WEDNESDAY—DECEMBER 4.

MR K. L. STADEL of Brandon, Florida, USA, sent me this story.

It seems that during the Gold Rush days an ambitious young man made a fabulous strike. A company was formed, machinery brought in and the mine started paying off in a big way. Then suddenly the rich vein disappeared. Months were spent trying to re-locate it, but finally they became discouraged and gave up.

The mine and equipment were sold to a junk man, but instead of scrapping the equipment the junk man brought in a mining specialist. A careful study of the rock formations convinced the specialist that the lost vein would be found only three feet from where the previous operation had stopped, and that is exactly what happened. The mine produced millions. The company had given up just three feet too soon.

The moral is obvious. If you're thinking of giving up—don't. The next push may be the one that does it!

CHARLES WESLEY, the great Methodist preacher and hymn-writer, was a happily married man, and although his preaching took him away from home for months on end, he had a way of keeping in close touch with his wife, Sally, across the dividing miles. They had promised each other to say a prayer at exactly the same time each day. Reminding her of this he once wrote in a letter from Ireland, "Remember to meet me always on Monday's noon and on each evening at five."

A thought, a prayer, a letter, a phone call—all these can vanquish the miles.

FRIDAY—DECEMBER 6.

MOST of us know of the work of the British and Foreign Bible Society in translating the Bible (or portions of it) into over a thousand different languages. I wonder if we ever stop to think of the skill and labour and patience involved in such work?

A good example of the difficulties which may be faced is in the story of the Borneo New Testament. The first translator was put to death during the Japanese occupation of Borneo during the Second World War, and then the whole enterprise was held up because the rest of the team had been made prisoners-of-war.

After the war the task was continued, but printing was impossible and it was to be another 15 long years before the people of Borneo had their first New Testament.

Perhaps we, too, when we take up our Bibles, might give a thought to the labour and love and patience and endurance which have gone into giving us God's Word.

THE FRIENDSHIP BOOK

WHILST lodging at a small farm, I was asked if I liked porridge. I said I did, but I was quite embarrassed next morning when I was the only person to be served a huge plateful. Of course I told the farmer's wife she should not have gone to so much trouble on my behalf.

"Oh, that was no trouble at all," she said cheerfully. "·I had to make it for the pig anyway!"

THEN he arose, and rebuked the wind and the raging of the water: and they ceased, and there was a calm.

THIS poem by P. J. Barsby captures the magic and beauty of a winter's day:

Snowflakes falling, soft and light
In the silence of the night.
In the morning, snow piled high;
Brilliant sunshine, clear blue sky.
Feathery trees on snowbound hill,
All around is calm and still.
In the distance, on the slopes,
Children sledging, hauling ropes.
Glistening snow on every hand
In this winter fairyland.
Then comes sunset's fiery glow
Tinting pink the crusted snow.
From the North a cold wind blows
Winter day draws to its close.
But in cottage, warm and bright,
A cheerful fire—a cosy night.

THE FRIENDSHIP BOOK

A FRIEND sent me this prayer which, he says, is ideal for anyone who leads a busy, crowded life:

" Slow me down, Lord! Give me amidst the confusion of my day the calmness of the everlasting hills. Break the tension of my nerves and muscles with the soothing music of the singing streams that live in my memory. Help me to know the magical restorative power of sleep. Give me the art of taking minute vacations—of slowing down to look at a flower, to chat to a friend, to pat a dog, to read a few lines of a good book.

" Slow me down, Lord, and inspire me to send my roots into the soil of life's enduring values, that I may grow towards the stars of my greater destiny."

RORY is five. This little redhead is the grandson of neighbours of ours. He often comes with us to the park, but the other day the Lady of the House and I intended to go farther than usual, so we had to say, " Sorry, Rory, but it's too far for you."

Rory wasn't to be beaten. " But I can go too far, too," he said with a determined look on his face. Of course we just couldn't refuse him after that!

As we set out we were still smiling at Rory's reply. But I couldn't help thinking how different the world would be, if some people—like Rory—hadn't been determined to go " too far ". Columbus wouldn't have discovered America, the Curies wouldn't have discovered radium and Hillary wouldn't have climbed Everest.

I am glad we took Rory. You'll be glad to know, too, that he was right—" too far " wasn't too far for him!

GIFTS

The earth has pleasure all our senses share:
The music of a stream, the scented air,
The clouds, the hills, the trees that greet our eyes,
Contribute to the memories we prize.

N

A MISSIONARY has told of a little native village in a clearing on the edge of the jungle where there were only a few Christians. The crowded huts and busy, noisy village often made it difficult for them to find a place for quiet prayer and meditation, so the custom grew for the Christians, one by one, to make their way through the long grass into the forest.

Soon, you could recognise a hut where a Christian lived because of the well-trodden path through the grass. If the quiet time was neglected, the path soon became overgrown again, and the missionary on his visit to the village, might say to one or other of the Christians, " Brother . . . sister . . . what has happened to your path?"

Many of us find our lives " overgrown " with worry and fear and weariness unless we take our own particular way of finding some means of stillness and quietness, whether it be through prayer, reading, listening to music or whatever else brings tranquillity back into our hearts.

H ENRY ROYCE, whose name is forever linked with that of his partner, Charles Rolls, in the motor car which bears their joint names, once said: " Strive for perfection in everything you do. Take the best that exists and make it better. When it does not exist, design it. Accept nothing nearly right or good enough."

Of course, Henry Royce was a genius (although he always described himself modestly as " mechanic "). Yet much of that idealism of his might well be applied in the humbler pursuits of our own lives with results that might astonish us.

THE FRIENDSHIP BOOK

I HAVE always been fascinated by place-names because their origin often gives some hint of a story connected with a town or village. Once, in the Malvern Hills, the Lady of the House and I came across Malvern Link. It has no particular claim to fame as has, say, its " big sister ", Great Malvern, but we were interested to find that the name originated in the old custom of linking extra horses to the stage-coaches for the climb up the steep hill to Great Malvern. That simple custom lives on in its name.

I couldn't help feeling that there are many people we know, with no claim to fame, who live on in our memory because at some time or other they have linked up with us in some simple act of help or encouragement to give us extra strength.

Wouldn't it be nice to think, too, that others remember *us* like that?

THEY that wait upon the Lord shall renew their strength; they shall mount up with wings as eagles; they shall run, and not be weary; and they shall walk, and not faint.

GATHERED round the fireside,
Telling tales of old,
Eager faces listening
To all the stories told.
No matter what the weather,
There's magic as you'll find—
When friends all meet together,
At jolly Christmastide!

TUESDAY—DECEMBER 17.

SOME time ago the Lady of the House and I stayed in an old farmhouse where we experienced that delight—all too rare in these days of central heating and smokeless zones—a log fire. For many of us there is a deep and lasting nostalgia about the glowing embers and the unforgettable smell of the burning wood.

But we were reminded, too, how, at this time of year, it used to be the custom to bring in and burn the Yule Log—a symbol, as the year drew to its close, of the burning up of old enmities and hatreds. What a good thing it would be if we all, at this season, resolved to do all within our power to " burn up " anything which spoils our human relationships and so help to fill our world with the fragrance of goodwill.

WEDNESDAY—DECEMBER 18.

THE diaries of the Rev Francis Kilvert give a fascinating account of the countryside and its people round about Clyro in the Wye Valley where he was a curate from 1865-72.

He tells of a visit he paid to a Rev. John Price, an eccentric old clergyman who virtually lived the life of a hermit. While not approving of the squalor in which the old man lived, Kilvert treasured a verse the hermit gave him written in a shorthand of his own invention:

A little health,
A little wealth,
A little house and freedom,
And at the end
A little friend
And little cause to need him.

. . . a simple philosophy, not without its value in our own busy, materialistic world.

HIS WORK

We plant and prune and weed and feed
  And give them our protection,
Yet know in higher power lies
  The source of their perfection.

THE FRIENDSHIP BOOK

I WONDER if sometimes, like me, you have wandered round an ancient church, leaflet or guide-book in hand, trying to identify the different parts and historical periods mentioned there. It isn't always easy, in spite of the guide-writer's help.

However, when the Lady of the House and I visited the parish church of Sherburn-in-Elmet in Yorkshire, which comprises work of several centuries from Norman times onward, we found that each age's contribution was neatly and unobtrusively labelled — " Fragment of 14th century arch ", " Clerestory 15th century " and so on.

History seemed to come alive for us in a new way. We ought, more often, to remember the good things which have come to us from the past and not just in our cultural heritage but in our own lives. We don't need labels—just a thankful prayer.

OUR friend Marguerite was concerned because she could not afford much in the way of Christmas presents. But, as we pointed out to her, she is already one of the greatest givers.

You see, Marguerite gives that most valuable commodity, time, to whoever happens to need it, all the year round. She listens with wisdom and kindness. Then she gives hope and courage and a spirit of enterprise. If it's practical help that is needed, Marguerite is the person everyone calls on. It only needs a ready smile from her to spread warmth and happiness, which you cannot buy and giftwrap.

I don't know whether we managed to convince our friend, but I think you'll agree —*real* giving has nothing at all to do with money.

THE FRIENDSHIP BOOK

DR NORMAN VINCENT PEALE, whose books have brought inspiration to countless people, tells of a holiday he spent in Switzerland in a chalet high in the mountains. It was a place of magnificent views but also of sudden and fierce storms.

He describes how " . . . the colossal storm breaks with heavy clouds, rolling fog, dashing rain, and thunder reverberating down the gorges of the Alps. But often, even in the midst of the storm's tumult, you may see, far away through a break in the clouds, a green mountainside bathed in sunlight. And you are encouraged that soon there will be fair skies again."

Just like life.

FOR unto you is born this day in the city of David a Saviour, which is Christ the Lord.

IN his book " Christmas ", about the customs of this festive season, William Sansom reminds us that when we sit down to our " traditional Christmas lunch " we shall probably " eat an Aztec bird against the background of an Alsatian tree, followed by a pudding spiced with tropical preserves, while one of our favourite carols is about the Bohemian King Wenceslas set to music taken from a Swedish Spring song."

And as we keep this feast in which so many different parts of the world are represented, let us pray that Christmas and all it stands for may bring hope to all the world.

L EWIS REDNER was a worried man. He had promised the children of the church of which he was organist that he would compose a tune for the words of a Christmas hymn which the minister had written. It was to be ready to be sung on the Sunday, but now it was Saturday evening and he still had not written a note. He went to bed feeling he had failed the whole congregation and let himself down.

However, during the night he was suddenly awakened by what he afterwards described as an " angel strain " ringing in his ear. He quickly jotted down the melody and on Sunday morning the tune was ready for the children to sing. Today it is one of our best-loved hymns: " O little town of Bethlehem ".

Lewis Redner always insisted that the music was a gift from Heaven.

WEDNESDAY—DECEMBER 25.

D ALE CARNEGIE, who helped thousands of people through his books " How to Win Friends and Influence People " and " How to Stop Worrying and Start Living ", came from a very poor home yet his mother and father managed, every year, to send money to an orphans' home in Iowa.

Carnegie said, " After I left home, I would always send Father and Mother a cheque at Christmas and urge them to indulge in a few luxuries for themselves. But they rarely did! When I came home for a few days before Christmas, Father would tell me of the coal and groceries they had bought for some ' widder woman ' in town who had a lot of children and no money to buy food and fuel. What joy they got out of these gifts—the joy of giving without accepting anything in return."

HOMEWARD BOUND

The sun gone down, the shadows fall,
A tiny breeze the wavelets chases,
Night coming on, a time to seek
Firelight and friendly faces.

THURSDAY—DECEMBER 26.

I LIKE this anonymous couplet:
> *If your face wants to smile, let it;*
> *If it doesn't, make it.*

FRIDAY—DECEMBER 27.

P. J. BARSBY of Attenborough, Nottingham, wrote these lines for New Year:

> *If we would all try hard each day*
> *to practise what we preach,*
> *To see each other's point of view*
> *and try to heal the breach*
> *Between ourselves and other folk*
> *who may be in the right,*
> *Extending hand of fellowship*
> *instead of fist to fight.*
> *If we would only try to smile*
> *when things are going wrong,*
> *And tackle our adversity*
> *with courage and a song.*
> *Then all the problems facing us*
> *would very soon recede,*
> *And we should find new happiness*
> *in helping those in need.*
> *So let us all this bright New Year*
> *remember every day*
> *To do our very best to help*
> *each other on life's way.*

SATURDAY—DECEMBER 28.

THE Greek philosopher Plato came out with this very astute piece of advice:
" When men speak ill of thee, live so that nobody will believe them."

SUNDAY—DECEMBER 29.

STRENGTHEN thee the weak hands, and confirm the feeble knees.

MONDAY—DECEMBER 30.

DOSTOYEVSKY, the Russian novelist, once wrote, " Love all God's creation, the whole and every grain of sand in it. Love every leaf, every ray of God's light. Love the animals, love the plants, love everything. If you love everything you will perceive the divine mystery in things. Once you perceive it you will begin to comprehend it better every day. And you will come at last to love the whole world with an all-embracing love."

Or, if you prefer it put a little more simply, " It's love that makes the world go round."

TUESDAY—DECEMBER 31.

WATCHNIGHT services, once so common on New Year's Eve, were popular with 18th century Methodists. Writing about such customs in 1861, J. Timbs said, " This Eve is called by the Wesleyan Methodists *Watch Night* because, at their principal chapels, the ministers and congregations hold a service to watch out the New Year, i.e. they pray until about five minutes to twelve o'clock, and then observe a profound silence until the clock strikes . . . "

Of course, there are happy and boisterous New Year celebrations in which we shall want to join, but how wise those old Methodists were to make provision, too, for silence—a few moments of recollection about the year which was passing and for contemplation of the year ahead.

Where the Photographs were taken

SEA SYMPHONY — *Dunnet Head, Caithness.*

WONDERLAND — *Old Basing, Hampshire.*

COUNTRY CANVAS — *Headley, Surrey.*

DAYBREAK — *River Windrush, Burford, Gloucestershire.*

ENDURING — *Widecombe-in-the-Moor, Devon.*

OASIS — *Flatford Mill, Suffolk.*

MIRACLE — *Selborne, near Alton, Hampshire.*

ALL ABOARD — *N. Warnborough, Hampshire.*

WANDERING — *Yelverton, Devon.*

ROOFS OF HOME — *Rockbourne, Hampshire.*

LEARNING YOUNG — *River Thames, Weybridge, Surrey.*

GRANDEUR — *Catrigg Force, N. Ribblesdale, Yorkshire.*

THANKS — *Oban, Argyll.*

REAL WEALTH — *Crook, Westmorland.*

CAREFREE — *Portland Bill, Dorset.*

GOLDEN AGE — *Cambridge.*

'MID THE FLOWERS — *Streatham, London.*

TIMELESS — *The Durdle Door, West Lulworth, Dorset.*

CONKER TIME — *South Inch, Perth.*

WOODLAND QUEEN — *Box Hill, Surrey.*

AT PLAY — *Sandown, Isle of Wight.*

JUST THINK . . . — *The Seven Sisters, East Sussex.*

GIFTS — *River Dee, Invercauld, Aberdeenshire.*

HOMEWARD BOUND — *Easdale, Argyll.*

Printed and Published by D. C. THOMSON & CO. LTD.,
185 Fleet Street, London EC4A 2HS.

ISBN 0 85116 318 1